GRANADA &
SAN JUAN DEL SUR

ELIZABETH PERKINS

Contents

Granada and Masaya

Look for ★ to find recommended sights, activities, dining, and lodging.

Highlights

© AVALON TRAVEL

★ **Iglesia La Merced:** Climb the bell tower for the best view in all of Granada (page 13).

★ **Las Isletas:** Spend a lazy day swimming, picnicking, and relaxing among hundreds of gorgeous islands (page 26).

★ **Zapatera Archipelago National Park:** These islands are rich in wildlife and historic artifacts (page 27).

★ **Volcán Mombacho:** More than a gorgeous photo-op, Volcán Mombacho has a first-class set of hiking trails, an eco-lodge, and a canopy tour (page 28).

★ **El Mercado Viejo Craft Market:** Handmade pottery, leatherwork, and paintings are all handsomely displayed in a market designed to showcase Nicaragua's finest crafts (page 32).

★ **Volcán Masaya National Park:** Peer into the gates of hell, wherein dwell demon parakeets, then visit the museum of this popular national park (page 37).

★ **Laguna de Apoyo:** Get away from it all in what might be the coolest swimming hole in the country: an enticing volcanic crater lake ringed with forest (page 40).

★ **Catarina Mirador:** This crater lip's patio terrace, with one of the best panoramas in Nicaragua, often offers live marimba music to accompany your beverage (page 43).

★ **San Juan de Oriente:** Visit this town of potters' workshops where you can observe ceramics being made and browse pre-Colombian style ceramic pieces (page 44).

★ **Carazo Beaches:** Lounge in natural pools found in huge rocks that line these beaches (page 48).

A ll within an hour of the capital, Granada, Masaya, and Carazo contain a taste of Nicaragua's must-sees. You'll find quaint colonial towns, smoking volcanoes, lagoons, traditional artistry, coffee farms, and the crashing tide of

the Pacific Ocean.

Granada's polished colonial architecture, horse-drawn carriages, and abundance of cafés, hotels, and spas—plus its strategic location—make it one of the country's most comfortable and popular spots for international visitors. Granada is a historical stronghold of conservatism. It is a striking juxtaposition of antique and modern, rich and poor, foreign and local. If you want to get a chocolate massage, eat a Middle Eastern dinner, and soak up some colonial charm, Granada is the place to go.

Just half an hour outside Managua, Masaya is a small town with a relaxed vibe. It's a city of artisans, metalworkers, leatherworkers, carpenters, painters, and musicians. In fact, no other region of Nicaragua is as blessed with a sense of artistry and creativity. Many of the handicrafts found in markets throughout the country are Masayan: hand-woven hammocks, terra-cotta pottery, musical instruments, and more. The charming Pueblos

Blancos, to the south and west of Masaya, are artisan villages. Make a day of pueblo hopping to visit workshops. In San Juan de Oriente you can watch a potter form a vase on a foot-spun wheel and buy pieces right out of the kiln for very reasonable prices. If you're eager to come home with something special, this is the place to find it.

Also outside Masaya are two must-see volcanic craters. Volcán Masaya is one of the world's most accessible volcanoes, one of only two on Earth where you can walk up to the crater lip and look inside. The region's most popular swimming hole, the Laguna de Apoyo, is a scenic 200-meter-deep crater lagoon. Lie on a floating dock, or kayak across it, surrounded by the sounds of birds and howler monkeys.

PLANNING YOUR TIME

There's a lot to see in this region. One day is enough time to see the major sites within the

Granada and Masaya

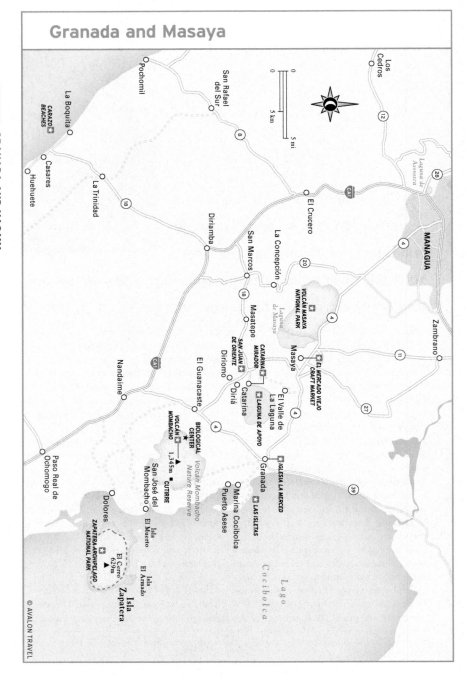

Los Cedros
Pochomil
San Rafael del Sur
La Boquita
CARAZO BEACHES
Casares
Huehuete
La Trinidad
Diriamba
San Marcos
La Concepción
El Crucero
MANAGUA
Laguna de Asososca
Zambrano
VOLCÁN MASAYA NATIONAL PARK
Laguna de Masaya
Masatepe
SAN JUAN DE ORIENTE
CATARINA MIRADOR
SAN JUAN DE ORIENTE
Diriomo
Masaya
EL MERCADO VIEJO CRAFT MARKET
El Valle de La Laguna
LAGUNA DE APOYO
Catarina
Diriá
El Guanacaste
Nandaime
VOLCÁN MOMBACHO
BIOLOGICAL CENTER
1,345m
Volcán Mombacho Nature Reserve
CUTIRRE
Granada
IGLESIA LA MERCED
LAS ISLETAS
San José del Mombacho
Paso Real de Ochomogo
Dolores
Isla El Muerto
Marina Cocibolca
Puerto Asese
ZAPATERA ARCHIPELAGO NATIONAL PARK
El Cerro 629m
Isla El Armado
Isla Zapatera
Lago Cocibolca

0   5 km
0   5 mi

© AVALON TRAVEL

city of Granada. A lot of the city's charm lies in the interesting excursions reachable using Granada as a base camp. Leave half a day for a boat ride in Las Isletas, and another day for Volcán Mombacho. Naturalists can easily spend a long day on hiking trails, in the visitor's center, and on guided tours.

Most travelers devote a day or so to visiting the pueblos and markets in and around Masaya. It's possible to make Masaya your base for excursions, though many travelers opt to stay in Granada, which has a much wider selection of hotels and restaurants that cater to tourists. While you could conceivably day-trip to the Laguna de Apoyo, the hotel options make it a fun place to stay overnight. (When was the last time you woke up inside a volcano crater?) Just an hour to the west are the Carazo beaches. Spend the day soaking up the sun and surf in La Boquita, or stay a night and let the waves lull you to sleep.

Public transportation is frequent in this region, and it's easy enough to hop on a bus to get where you need to go. However, renting a car is a must if you're short on time.

Granada

Arguably Nicaragua's most picturesque town, Granada is an easy place to love. Much of its colonial architecture is remarkably intact and is being painstakingly restored. The colorful facades lining old narrow streets practically glow in the late afternoon sun. It's sultry and tropical here, and a fresh breeze blows off the waters of Lake Cocibolca. The views from along the lakeshore's broad, undeveloped shoreline—and the ever-looming silhouette of Volcán Mombacho—make for easy photos and good memories. At night the sky fills with stars and the neighbors come out to chitchat on their front stoops; inside even the most nondescript colonial facade is an open, private courtyard designed to capture the evening breeze.

See Granada from a horse-drawn carriage.

Granada

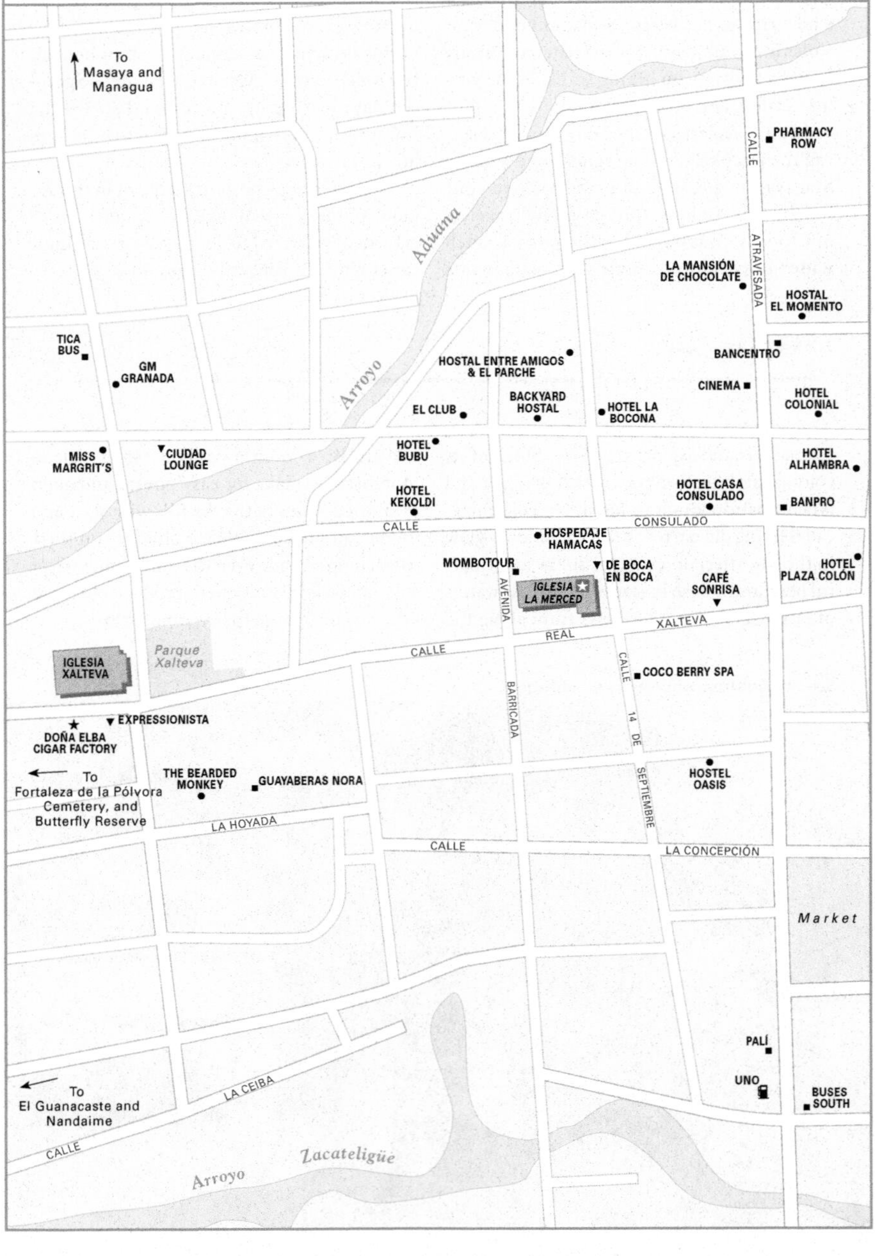

To
Masaya and
Managua

CALLE

PHARMACY
ROW

ATRAVESADA

LA MANSIÓN
DE CHOCOLATE

HOSTAL
EL MOMENTO

Aduana

Arroyo

TICA
BUS

GM
GRANADA

HOSTAL ENTRE AMIGOS
& EL PARCHE

BANCENTRO

EL CLUB

BACKYARD
HOSTAL

CINEMA

HOTEL LA
BOCONA

HOTEL
COLONIAL

MISS
MARGRIT'S

CIUDAD
LOUNGE

HOTEL
BUBU

HOTEL
ALHAMBRA

HOTEL
KEKOLDI

HOTEL CASA
CONSULADO

BANPRO

CALLE

CONSULADO

HOSPEDAJE
HAMACAS

MOMBOTOUR

DE BOCA
EN BOCA

CAFÉ
SONRISA

HOTEL
PLAZA COLÓN

IGLESIA
LA MERCED

XALTEVA

AVENIDA

REAL

*Parque
Xalteva*

CALLE

CALLE

COCO BERRY SPA

IGLESIA
XALTEVA

BARRICADA

14 DE

EXPRESSIONISTA

DOÑA ELBA
CIGAR FACTORY

To
Fortaleza de la Pólvora
Cemetery, and
Butterfly Reserve

THE BEARDED
MONKEY

GUAYABERAS NORA

HOSTEL
OASIS

SEPTIEMBRE

LA HOYADA

CALLE

LA CONCEPCIÓN

Market

PALÍ

UNO

To
El Guanacaste and
Nandaime

LA CEIBA

BUSES
SOUTH

CALLE

Arroyo

Zacateligüe

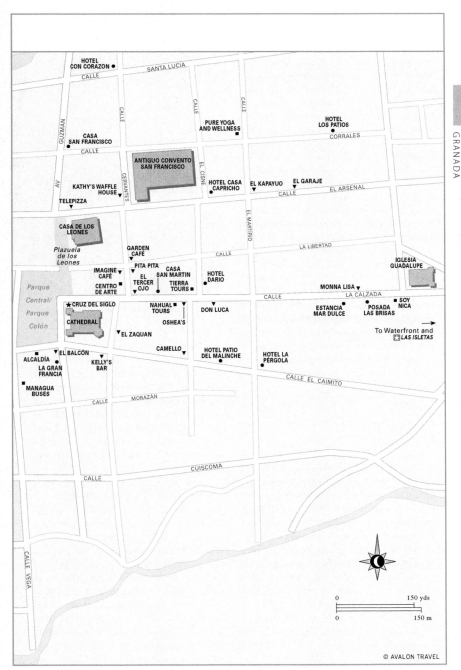

© AVALON TRAVEL

ORIENTATION

From Granada's central tree-lined plaza, a.k.a. the Parque Central and Parque Colón, look south to the giant Volcán Mombacho. Just behind the cathedral on the park's east side, Calle La Calzada runs due east about one kilometer to the municipal dock on the lake. A lot of the lodging and restaurants lie along this street or within a block or two of it.

At the lake, a paved road runs south along the water's edge to the *malecón* (waterfront), a tourist complex that's emptier than it should be due to its tendency to attract thieves (it's not a good idea to walk around a lot in this area). An easy taxi ride farther south are the marinas that provide boat access to Las Isletas and Zapatera.

West of the plaza is the Xalteva (pronounced, more or less, with a hard "h") neighborhood and eventually the cemetery and road to Nandaime. In this neighborhood, one block west of the Plaza, is Calle Atravesada, running north-south between the old 1886 train station and the bustling chaos of the municipal market. This is one of Granada's main thoroughfares and a modern commercial center for banks, movie theaters, and the like.

SIGHTS

Parque Colón (Central Plaza) and Cathedral

If Granada is the center of tourism in Nicaragua, then Granada's central plaza is the heart of it all. You'll pass through here dozens of times during your stay in Granada, and each time, sweat-drenched, you'll pause for something cold to drink. People-watchers will find it hard to leave, as the park is a steady stream of students gossiping, elderly men playing chess, and vendors hawking carved wooden toys, ceramics, jewelry, ice cream, and more. Order a glass of icy *fresco de cacao* at one of the corner kiosks, and enjoy the raucous bird-chatter in the treetops and the hustle and bustle of life in North America's first colonial city.

Cross the park to the magnificent

Granada's cathedral sits in the heart of the city.

cathedral on the plaza's east side. It's sometimes open to the public (even the bell towers). When the doors open for mass, it's worth a peek inside. The stone and wooden interior is dim and cool, and the bells echo overhead. Just outside the church's front step is the Cruz del Siglo (Century Cross), inaugurated January 1, 1900. Entombed in its cement are coins, pieces of art, and a gilded bottle from the 19th century.

La Plazuela de los Leones

The pedestrian space guarded by the cannon off the northeast corner of the main plaza is where Henry Morgan once set 18 cannons during his sacking of the city, and where, a century later, William Walker (the U.S. filibuster who once burned the city to the ground) was sworn in as President of Nicaragua. On the Plazuela's eastern side is the Casa de los Leones, a colonial-era home whose lush interior has been transformed into an international cultural center. Don Diego de Montiel, governor of Costa Rica, built the

Casa de los Leones in 1720. William Walker did not miss the opportunity to burn this place down, leaving nothing standing but the portal bearing the Montiel family crest (still visible). The unique, neoclassical colonnade facade was a product of the subsequent reconstruction. In 1987, the historical monument became the headquarters of the Casa de los Tres Mundos Foundation (tel. 505/2552-4176, www.c3mundos.org, daily 8am-6pm), bearing an art and music school, museum, historical archive, library, concert hall, literary café, bookstore, and exhibition space that hosts resident artists from around the world.

Antiguo Convento San Francisco

The Antiguo Convento San Francisco (1 block north and 2 east of the main cathedral, tel. 505/2552-5535, Mon.-Fri. 8am-5pm, Sat.-Sun. 9am-4pm, $2) and its trio of bells were once famously blue. Inside, set around open courtyards festooned with palm trees are centuries' worth of priceless artwork and 30 alter-ego statues collected a century ago from Zapatera Island. The carved basalt shows human forms with the heads of jaguars, birds, and crocodiles whose spirits were thought to flow through humans' souls—a rare look into the cosmology of Nicaragua's pre-Columbian peoples. There is also a large, to-scale replica of the city, and exhibits that represent the lifestyle of the Chorotega and Nahautl peoples. The convent was first built by Franciscan monks in 1529 and lasted 150 years before pirate Henry Morgan burned it to the ground. Since then it has housed William Walker's troops, U.S. Marines, a contingent of engineers surveying a possible canal route in the 1920s, and the National University.

Calle La Calzada

Walk east from Parque Colón toward the lake along Granada's hippest strip, recently reworked with a modern pedestrian-friendly design, but with an old feel featuring cobblestones, street lamps, and wide sidewalks. Halfway to the lake, stop at the 17th-century Iglesia de Guadalupe, first built in 1626 and most recently refurbished in 1945. Continuing along the palm-lined boulevard, you'll reach the *muelle* and *malecón* (dock and waterfront) on the water's edge.

The Waterfront

At the lakeshore where the Calzada ends, stop and take in Granada's lacustrine panorama. Turn right and pass through "the rooks" (a pair of statues) to enter the Centro Turístico, a short row of restaurants and discos lining the lakeshore. This area has become attractive to robbers in the past few years and is often overrun with chayules (almost invisible biting water flies). Somehow this place fails to live up to its potential; it's not even good for swimming. From here, however, you can catch a cab south to where the boats depart for tours of the *isletas*.

★ Iglesia La Merced

Built in 1534, sacked and burned by Henry Morgan in 1670, then rebuilt, the church itself is pretty, located on the northeast corner of the intersection of the Calle Real and Avenida 14 de Septiembre. Ascend the tight spiral stairs of the bell tower (daily 10am-6pm, $1) for the single most spectacular view in the city. Look over an ocean of tiled roofs to the lake and *isletas,* with Volcán Mombacho over your shoulder. The scene changes over the course of the day; late afternoons are best when the shadows are long.

Fortaleza de la Pólvora and Cemetery

Built in 1748 to secure Granada's gunpowder supply from marauding pirates, La Pólvora's (7 blocks west of La Merced, free) medieval architecture speaks of simplicity and strength: five squat towers and one heavily guarded gate with two oak doors. In the 20th century, both the city government and later Somoza's National Guard used the old fort and powder storage facility as a military garrison, and later a jail. These days it's a museum of arms or art whose exhibitions rotate regularly. Climb the towers for a breath of wind and a good perspective of the skyline, but watch your head and your step. Adjacent, the 10-meter-high arched stone walls known as **Los Muros de Xalteva** were erected by the Spaniards in the mid-1700s to separate Spanish settlements from those of the locals. There is a relaxing park across the street with interesting stone shapes.

Located at Granada's southwest corner, Granada's **cemetery** of enormous marble tombs—bigger than the homes of many Nicaraguans—shelters the bones of several centuries of elite from Granada's heyday, including a half-dozen presidents. Note the column-lined Capilla de Animas and the replica of the Magdalena de Paris, both built between 1876 and 1922.

Butterfly Reserve

At the **Nicaragua Butterfly Reserve** (2 kilometers down the dirt road to the right of the cemetery, tel. 505/8895-3012, nicaraguabutterflyreserve.wordpress.com, $5) tour the flight house filled with a magical array of butterfly species. You can also stroll around the grounds of this lush old fruit orchard. From the cemetery, it's 45 minutes on foot, or take a bicycle or pay $1 for a *moto* taxi.

RECREATION
Spas and Massage

The three blind masseuses at **Seeing Hands Massage** (Calle La Calzada in Hospital La Calzada and Calle 14 de Septiembre, across from Barba del Mono, tel. 505/8671-9770, massageseeinghands.blogspot.com, Mon.-Sat. 9am-5:30pm, 15-minute chair massage $5, 1-hour table massage $15) will give you a chair or full body massage. **Coco Berry Spa** (Calle 14 de Septiembre half a block south of the Iglesia La Merced, tel. 505/8466-6507, cocoberryspa.com, $30-40) is a full service spa that makes imaginative products using local products like cacao (don't miss the chocolate massage!) and volcanic clay. Their prices are extremely reasonable considering the quality of their products. **Pure Yoga and Wellness Retreats** (Calle Corrales, 1.5 blocks east of the Convento San Francisco, tel. 505/2552-2304, Purenica.com, daily) is a full service gym and yoga studio that has a variety of exercise and yoga classes as well as spa treatments. It's also home to a gigantic tortoise.

Boating and Swimming

Getting out on the water is the right way to enjoy this beautiful corner of Nicaragua.

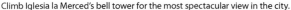

Climb Iglesia la Merced's bell tower for the most spectacular view in the city.

Taking a boat trip through the *isletas* is the best way to do that. Vladimir Torrez (at the end of the Centro Turístico Puerto Las Piedras Pintadas, tel. 505/8380-8196, tjorgevladimir@yahoo.com, $10/hour guided kayak tour, $20-40/hour boat tour, discounts for longer tours) is a recommended *lanchero* (boat operator), hired by many of the tour operators for his kayaks and motorboats. Vladimir and his team offer a variety of tour options. Inuit Kayaks (Centro Turístico, tel. 505/8691-0616, 2.5 hours minimum, $25/hour) rents kayaks.

The stand-up paddleboard trend has made it to Nicaragua and there are a few companies doing paddleboard tours of the *isletas*. Livit Tours (tel. 505/8085-7014, www.livit-water.com, $34-39, reservations must be made 24-hours ahead of time) is a company specializing in paddleboarding whose tours and paddleboard yoga classes leave from El Tercer Ojo restaurant twice a day.

To beat the heat, use the swimming pool at the Mombacho Beach Club (Calle Atravesada, across from Bancentro, tel. 505/2552-4678, daily 10am-6pm, $5), located inside Mansión de Chocolate. You can make spa and beauty appointments there as well, and these entitle you to use the pool. Swim laps, cool off, enjoy cocktails and light snacks, or check email in a chic atmosphere.

Bicycling

While biking around the city center can be complicated if you haven't oriented yourself first, there are plenty of other places to trek around town, including along the *malecón*. It's best to start early before the temperature rises. A bike ride down the Peninsula de Asese can be excellent, and the birdlife present there is astounding. In town, you can rent bikes at Nahuatl Tours (1 block down from the central square, tel. 505/8889-2461, nahualtours.com, $1/hr or $7/day) or, closer to the waterfront, NicarAgua Dulce (Marina Cocibolca, tel. 505/8802-0285, www.nicaraguadulce.com), where you can rent a beater bike. De Tours (Calle Corrales house #305,

northern side of the San Francisco Convent, tel. 505/2552-0155, www.detour-nicaragua.com), a tour operation committed to avoiding the use of fossil fuels, runs lots of bike trips to nearby sites and towns.

ENTERTAINMENT AND EVENTS
Bars and Clubs

There are three pub-style bars that are always full of traveler types on weekends. Reilly's Irish Tavern (Calle la Libetad, 1 block west of the Calzada, next to Imagine Café, tel. 505/7706-4157, daily from 9am) is probably the most popular bar among travelers. They have lots of themed nights and promotions as well as the best wings in town. O'Sheas Irish Pub (right on the Calzada, tel. 505/8454-1140 www.osheas-nicaragua.com, daily 8:30am-2am) is an Irish-owned pub that serves food and smoothies all day, and is a packed bar at night. Their specialty drink is the Jäger Thom (named after the owner), a dangerous combination of whisky, Jäger, and Redbull, served aflame. Kelly's Bar (Calle Caimito, 1 block east off of the Calzada, tel. 505/2552-2430, daily) is a sports bar turned club on the weekends. On Saturdays expect a $7-12 cover and an open bar.

A more romantic lounge scene can be found at El Tercer Ojo (Calle El Arsenal across from Convento San Francisco, tel. 505/2552-6451, Tues.-Sun. 11am-11pm). Try their swank tapas, wine, cocktails, and more. It's especially popular during happy hour (4pm-7pm). They are also now selling kombucha.

El Balcón (southeast corner of the central plaza, tel. 505/2552-6002, daily noon-10pm), on the second floor of the grand yellow-painted Gran Francia, offers the best aerial street-side balcony from which to watch the foot and horse traffic below as you sip your Centenario and enjoy the delicious bar menu.

Managua is better for dancing, but a tiny club scene exists in Granada. Casual and a little rowdy, Inuit Bar (inside the Centro Turístico, 505/8661-7655, Fri. and Sat. only)

Volunteering in Granada

If you can commit more than a couple of weeks and have decent Spanish, you can turn your vacation into something more than just travel by volunteering with one of several Granada-based organizations. Yes, you'll miss out on some hammock time, but look at what you'll gain:

Building New Hope (BNH) (U.S. tel. 412/421-1625, in Granada, call Donna Tabor at tel. 505/8852-0210, www.buildingnewhope.org), based in both Granada and Pittsburgh, Pennsylvania, is a nonprofit organization providing a number of ongoing programs with volunteer opportunities. BNH manages two neighborhood schools that welcome volunteer teachers' assistants. They assist the community library and reading-in-schools program (contact Carol Ann Rae). BNH is also on the lookout for music teachers for their Rhythm in the Barrios project (requires intermediate Spanish and one-month minimum commitment).

Empowerment International (519 Calle Libertad, tel. 505/2552-1653, U.S. tel. 303/823-6495, www.empowermentinternational.org) runs a community-based educational program for impoverished and at-risk youth. Direct work with the families and community is an integral part of their methodology, as are art and photography projects. They serve Villa Esperanza and Santa Ana de Malacos, two outlying communities of Granada. Intermediate Spanish is a must.

Hogar Madre Albertina (from Colegio Padre Misieri, 2 blocks north, hogardeninasmadrealbertina.com) is an underfunded home for girls where volunteers are sometimes welcome to read to or play games with the girls and help them with their homework. A one-month minimum stay and intermediate Spanish are required.

La Harmonía (Carraterra Masaya, 2 blocks west of La Colonia supermarket, eeap_aman@yahoo.com) is an organization for mentally and physically challenged children and young adults. They accept volunteers with basic Spanish who can teach handicrafts, weaving, haircutting, sign language, or have experience in special education.

La Esperanza Granada (Calle Libertad #307, tel. 505/8934-2273 or 8913-8946, www.la-esperanza-granada.org, info@la-esperanza-granada.org) focuses on education, especially with young children. Volunteers work in public schools on the outskirts of Granada; they tutor and teach arts and crafts, sports, English, and more. There is volunteer housing ($23/week) in the center of Granada; a one-month minimum stay and intermediate Spanish is preferred. They also have lots of experience with groups of international volunteers for short-term projects.

serves cold beer amidst reggaeton music. WEEKEND (in the Centro Turístico, tel. 505/8581-9549, Thurs.-Sun. $3-5 cover) is the trendiest club in town with live DJs and electronic music played at high volume. Make sure to take a taxi both ways and do not walk in this part of town at night.

Festivals and Events

A concerted effort to raise Granada's profile, the annual Poetry Festival (Feb.) is a knockout, drawing not only Nicaragua's most acclaimed literati and musicians (Gioconda Belli, Ernesto Cardenal, Norma Elena Gadea), but an astonishing array of poets and artists from around the world as well. The event capitalizes on the open spaces of several Granada landmarks, including cathedrals, the San

Francisco convent, and Granada's best plazas. If your trip coincides with this event, book your room early.

Berrinche Ambiental (Jan.) is another great festival that takes place in Granada. The programming focuses on youth and people who have "youthful spirits," using art, mime, and celebration to promote artistic expression and environmental consciousness. They offer lots of workshops and performances and always attract an international crowd.

Throughout the rest of the year, the Casa de los Leones (east side of Plazuela de los Leones, tel. 505/2552-4176) sponsors frequent events, including concerts by local musicians and visiting international artists. Imagine Café (tel. 505/2552-4672, imaginerestaurantandbar.com) is a restaurant in town that often has live music. Check their Facebook page (Imagine Restaurant and Bar) for upcoming events. Granada's humble movie theater, El Teatro Karawala (1 block west of the plaza), offers popular (often trashy) American movies.

SHOPPING

Though Masaya is the place most people look for artisan crafts, Granada offers a few unique shopping opportunities. There are several gift shops around the plaza, as well as frequent street vendors. The municipal market (1 block south of the plaza) spills up Calle Atravesada and is geared more for locals than tourists, but it is lots of fun to visit.

Cooperative El Parche Gift Shop (halfway down the block north of the Piedra Bocona, Calle 14 de Septiembre, tel. 505/8473-7700) is a cooperative store where local artisans display their products. While the products you find in many markets are often similar, this store has truly unique and creative items often made out of recycled products and local materials. A portion of their proceeds goes to doing workshops in rural communities on recyclable art and other techniques.

Soy Nica (Calle La Calzada in front of Carlos Bravo School, tel. 505/2552-0234, www.soynica.dk, Mon.-Thurs. 9am-6pm, Fri.-Sun. 9am-10pm) uses Nicaraguan leather to make stylish bags and other leather goods in a wide variety of colors. The workshop is right there in the store and you can stop in to see the process of working the leather.

Along the Calzada are a handful of boutiques selling clothes and accessories. Centro de Arte (Calle la Calzada, turn left 1 block from the Parque Colón, tel. 505/2552-6461, www.nicaragua-art.com, daily 6am-9pm) is an art gallery and store, which features pieces by local and international artists. You can also take art classes (from $6, come before 9am to sign up, children's classes on Sat.) and enjoy a coffee or sandwich at their Café de Arte.

Granada is *guayabera* country, and there are several places to buy these elegant Latin shirts. The best (and most expensive) shop is Guayabera Nora (east side of the Parque Central right around the corner from the Bearded Monkey, tel. 505/2552-4617). At Sultan Cigars (on Calle Vega across from the Plaza Central, tel. 505/8803-9569, eddyreyes78@yahoo.es, daily 8am-7pm), Eddy Reyes and family can make you a custom labeled case (your name on a cigar label) in a couple of hours; otherwise visit Doña Elba Cigar Factory (1 block west of Iglesia Xalteva, tel. 505/8860-6715, daily 7am-7pm). Antique lovers will adore Casa de Antiguedades (1 block north of Parque Colón on Calle Arsenal, tel. 505/8874-2034, haroldsandino@hotmail.com).

ACCOMMODATIONS

Granada lodging runs from youthful backpacker hostels to boutique-refurbished colonial homes. Much of the accommodations are located conveniently near Central Plaza. Interestingly, recent years have seen huge turnover in expat-owned places that appeared at the start of the real estate boom but then disappeared without a whisper. Locally owned places have mostly weathered the storm. Expect higher rates during the high season (Dec.-Apr.).

Under $25

★ Hostel El Momento (Calle el Aresenal 104, tel. 505/8457-6560, www.hotelgranadanicaragua.com, $8 dorm, $14-42 private) is the cleanest, most relaxed hostel around. They have new beds, trendy and comfortable common areas, a bar and restaurant, Wi-Fi, iPads available for use, laundry service, and they offer tours. The most hopping backpacker joint is a new place called Backyard Hostal (2 blocks west of Parque Colón on Calle Libertad, tel. 505/89842490, $7 dorm, $16-20 private). This place has a vibe of a backyard college party. They have a pool and a bar that are busy all day. They also have themed nights (movie nights, beer-pong tournaments) and offer tours. There is an open kitchen and a small food stand across the street where you can buy food to prepare.

Community Tourism near Granada

For those seeking a full-immersion cultural experience, the most obvious option is to sign up for a homestay with one of the many Spanish schools in Granada. This is a good option if you want to stay with a Nicaraguan family and still have access to Granada's many restaurants, Internet cafés, and other distractions. If you'd really like to get out there, consider arranging a few days (or weeks) with the **Unión de Cooperativas Agropecuarias Tierra y Agua,** also known as the **Earth and Water UCA** (Granada office: 75 yards west of the Shell Palmira, tel. 505/2552-0238, www.ucatierrayagua.org, turismo@ucatierrayagua.org, Mon.-Fri. 9am-4pm, $5/night pp, $3/meal). The UCA is an association of rural farmers on the slopes of Volcán Mombacho and Isla de Zapatera National Park who will be glad to be your hosts. You'll stay in simple Nicaraguan lodging in La Granadilla or Zonzapote and eat typical food while getting to know a rural community. Local guides will take you horseback riding, hiking, fishing, and more. Cheap transport to and from Granada can be arranged. Income generated by your visit goes directly to a cooperative collective fund to pay for meals, guides, maintenance, etc., and to distribute to families involved. The UCA maintains a general fund for tourism, used for training and to make small loans for tourist-related projects.

GM Granada (in front of the Tica Bus Station, tel. 505/2552-2910 or 8962-9954, gm-granada.com, GM@GMGranada.com, $11-30) is particularly popular for travelers coming up from Costa Rica on Tica Bus. This hostel is farther out of town than some of the other options (a 10-minute walk from the center), but this also gives it a calm vibe that some other hostels lack. Unlike some of its sloppy competitors, the pristine white walls and a clean blue pool give this place a sharp presentation. **Hospedaje Hamacas** (Calle El Consulado, 250 meters west of Parque Colón, tel. 505/2552-0679, hostalhamacasgranada.com, $5 dorm, $8-15 private with a/c) is a locally owned basic hostel at a great price. They are owned together with Nahuatl Tours. **Hostal Entre Amigos** (half block north of the Piedra Bocona on Calle 14 de Septiembre, tel. 505/8473-7700, hostalentreamigos.com, $5-25) is a small, laid-back hostel whose reception doubles as the **Cooperative El Parche Gift Shop.** They have special rates for people volunteering in Granada and also offer volunteer opportunities with their cooperative artisan shop. **Hostel Oasis** (1 block north, 1 block east of the local market, tel. 505/2552-8005, www.nicaraguahostel.com, $9 dorm, $20-45 private) is a laid-back place with a small swimming pool and a nice garden.

Past the restaurants of La Calzada are a handful of locally owned hostels whose locations can't be beat and are simple and economical. **Posada las Brisas** (Calle la Calzada, tel. 505/2552-3984 or 8885-3989, tcristac@hotmail.es, $12-20) is family-run, safe, and clean. Its features include wireless Internet, refrigerator, and kitchen access and fans, but no air-conditioning.

$25-50

Granada's midrange and upscale hotels offer remarkable value, each striving to offer an authentic but unique colonial experience with all the amenities. In this price range and above you can usually expect breakfast to be included as well as hot water, air-conditioning, private bathrooms, cable TV, artsy decor, and the ubiquitous open-air central patio with small swimming pool.

★ **Hotel Kekoldi** (3.5 blocks west of Parque Colón on Calle El Consulado, tel. 506/2252-4006, U.S. tel. 786/221-9011, www.kekoldi-nicaragua.com, Granada@kekoldi-nicaragua.com, $41-65) is spacious and colorful with well-planned architecture and plenty of open spaces. The pool is small, but the rooms are decorated with beautiful mosaics. Expect to find your towels folded into creative pieces of art.

Hotel La Pérgola (3 blocks east of Parque Colón on Calle El Caimito, tel. 505/2552-4221, www.lapergola.com.ni, info@lapergola.com.ni, $35-55) has 26 rooms with private baths and access to a gorgeous open balcony (for which the hotel is named), plus tour service and Wi-Fi.

Estancia Mar Dulce (Calle la Calzada, 3.5 blocks east of Parque Colón, tel. 505/2552-3732, www.hotelmardulcenicaragua.com, granadamardulce@hotmail.com, $30 without a/c, $40-55 private) is locally owned, clean, and professional. It has large, pleasant rooms and a spacious interior courtyard with a landscaped swimming pool.

El Club (3 blocks west of the northwest corner of Parque Colón, tel. 505/2552-4245, www.elclub-nicaragua.com, $30-90, includes continental breakfast) has a modern look with cozy, smaller rooms. They have a new whirlpool tub and there is a two-floor mezzanine room great for families. Hotel Casa San Martín (Calle La Calzada, 1 block east of the park, tel. 505/2552-6185, www.hcasasanmartin.com, reservaciones@hcasasanmartin.com, $41-66) has eight rooms, all with attractive hardwood floors.

For a nearby break 20 minutes north of the city, try Hacienda los Malacos (tel. 505/8485-3959, losmalacos.com, $35 pp dorm, $80 pp private room), a private nature reserve and eco-hotel, which offers all-inclusive hotel options and day trips. You can tour this farm/reforestation project on foot, on a bike, or on horseback and there is also great bird-watching and row boating on the properties.

$50-100

Run by a couple of dynamic and well-traveled ex-Peace Corps volunteer sisters, ★ Casa San Francisco (cattycorner to the Convento San Francisco, tel. 505/2552-8235, www.casasanfrancisco.com, csfgranada@yahoo.com, $55-95) is a charming colonial cluster of 19 decorated rooms. It features a small pool and is located in a quiet and central neighborhood. You'll also find a great on-site restaurant and bar called Bocadillos that specializes in tapas.

La Mansión de Chocolate (in front of Bancentro on Calle Atrevesada, tel. 505/25524678, mansiondechocolate.com, $80-200) is located inside Granada's largest intact colonial mansion (formerly known as Hotel Spa Granada). The beautiful house has been decorated using quirky architectural furniture, which creates an interesting juxtaposition. The pool is luxurious (watch out for the gang of ducks, they do not like to be touched). The hotel's spa, despite lack of trained masseuses, has interesting treatments, like the chocolate massage. The hotel also houses the Choco Café and Museum, which has an all-you-can-eat breakfast buffet and workshops on how cacao becomes chocolate.

With a feeling more like a private colonial mansion than a hotel, Miss Margrit's (2 blocks north of the Xalteva Park, look for a small sign, tel. 505/8983-1398, missmargrits.com, missmargrits@gmail.com, $70-90) is a beautifully restored home with seven rooms. It is located farther away from the center of town than other options, but comes highly recommended. Whether lounging by the pool, getting a massage, bathing in your jungle-like bathroom (some of the rooms have a garden inside), or playing billiards, you are guaranteed to feel pampered.

Hotel Patio del Malinche (Calle El Caimito, 2.5 blocks east of the central plaza, tel. 505/2552-2235, www.patiodelmalinche.com, $75-95) is a stunning restored home whose owners have taken a lot of care in collecting tasteful decorations and promoting local artisans. Sixteen rooms surround a huge patio, bar, and pool.

Hotel Casa Consulado (Calle el Consulado #105, 30 meters west of Banpro, tel. 505/2552-2709, U.S. 305/704-2078, info@hconsulado.com, $75-110) is a luxurious-feeling colonial building with bright colored walls and a pleasant pool and fountains. It has huge rooms with tile floors, some of which have lofts. This is a great space for families.

Hotel Casa Capricho (Calle El Arsenal, a block east of Convento San Francisco, tel. 505/2552-8422, www.hotecasacapricho.com,

$50-120), with nine rooms, an open kitchen, a dining room, and common areas is ideal for families. It's colorful and pleasant.

★ **Hotel con Corazón** (Calle Santa Lucia 141, tel. 505/2552-8852, www.hotelconcorazon.com, $60-100) has Scandinavian styling and works for a cause. In addition to the hotel, this is a foundation that invests heavily in the community, particularly in education. They have a charming little pool, 16 comfortable rooms, and a large swing. They also offer salsa classes.

Hotel Alhambra (northwest corner of the central plaza, tel. 505/2552-4486, www.hotelalhambragranda.com, $57-120) was Granada's first luxury hotel and has the best location in town, right on the park. Built around a pleasing landscaped patio, its 56 newly remodeled rooms (some with superb balcony views) have exposed wood beams and are tastefully decorated. The whole place has a classy, mahogany-enhanced ambience. ★ **Hotel Colonial** (20 meters west of the park's northwest corner, tel. 505/2552-7299, hotelcoloialgranada.com, $70-120) is newer, with 37 clean, well-appointed rooms (some including whirlpool tub) surrounding an outdoor patio, pool, and bar.

Staying at the ★ **Hotel La Bacona** (Calle La Libertad, 2 blocks west of the park, www.hotellabocona.com, hotelbocona@yahoo.com, tel. 505/2552-2888, $80-140) gives guests the feeling of living in colonial Granada. Each room has exquisite period furniture, cathedral ceilings, and ornate wooden doors, as well as four-poster king-size beds with luxurious draping. There are no TVs in the rooms and, in order to maintain the integrity of the building, the bathrooms are located outside of the rooms. The hotel also has modern amenities: a huge pool, Wi-Fi access, and an on-site spa. Half of La Bacona's profits are donated to a local NGO, La Carita Feliz, which has youth programming and serves free meals to thousands of local children.

Hotel Dario (3 blocks east of the central park, tel. 505/2552-3400, www.hoteldario.com, $90-104) has open walkways, gardens, and 22 rooms that make artful use of the available space. Request one of the rooms with small balconies facing Mombacho.

Over $100

A restored colonial mansion, the brand-new **Hotel Bubu** (Calle Libertad, from the BAC bank, 2.5 blocks west, tel. 505/2552-3432, hotelbubu.com, $140-160) has a modern design. Situated around a 13-meter lap pool, its five junior suites were built with every detail promoting airflow in order to avoid the need for air-conditioning. This hotel feels luxurious and exclusive; the second-floor terrace has a panoramic view of Granada where you can have a private breakfast or invite friends over for drinks. An intimate boutique hotel, **Hotel Los Patios** (Calle Corrales 525, tel. 505/25520641, lospatiosgranada.com, $90-175) features a range of indoor/outdoor spaces with a modern, minimalist Scandinavian design. Los Patios has five spacious rooms with beautiful tile floors. Its outdoor spaces feature a pool, green area, and giant chessboard. With a chic modern kitchen for guest use in the center, this hotel really feels like your own personal mansion.

One of Granada's first buildings (and one of a few that withstood the fire that consumed the rest of the city in the days of William Walker) has been painstakingly restored as ★ **La Gran Francia Hotel y Restaurante** (southeast corner of the park, tel. 505/2552-6000, www.lagranfrancia.com, $110-157). A careful blend of neoclassical and colonial elements in hardwoods, wrought iron, and porcelain characterize La Gran Francia's every detail, down to the hand-painted sinks.

Hotel Plaza Colón (on the west side of the park, tel. 505/2552-8489, www.hotelplazacolon.com, $109-234) has 26 large, elegant rooms with air-conditioning, hot water, cable TV, and ceiling fan; 6 rooms have vast wooden porches looking straight across the central plaza to the main cathedral, a beautiful (but sometimes noisy) vista. The other rooms face a quiet street or the sculpted inner courtyards and pool. A restaurant, bar, and wine cellar are on the premises, and parking is available.

FOOD

The Granada dining scene is in constant rotation, with old favorites disappearing, new contenders, and creative experimentation. Here are some favorite picks, but you won't go hungry if you simply stroll around.

The two major **supermarkets** are the **Palí** (on Calle Atravesada just south of the market) and **La Colonial** (from the Puma market, 1 block west) both open daily until 8pm or so. The local **market** (1 block south of the plaza) is a great place to buy fruits and veggies during the day. As many of the lower-priced *hospedajes* offer a kitchen and fridge, you can stretch your travel dollars immensely by using these markets.

Fritanga and Local Fare

Asados Don Chilo (in front of the cemetery, tel. 505/2553-4934, $5) is the best place in town for an authentic Nicaraguan meal. This buffet specializes in grilled meats served to you in a plantain leaf along with fried sweet or green plantains and cabbage salad.

Las Colinas Sur (from the Shell Palmira, 1 block south, 1 block towards the lake, tel. 505/2552-3492 or 505/8883-1522, $10-20) is a dirt floor rancho popular among locals for a nice meal with the family. They have all sorts

of Nicaraguan cuisine but their specialty is *guapote,* a fish caught in Lake Cocibolca. The restaurant is outside the center of town, so it might be best to take a cab.

In Granada, there are a handful of *fritangas*—roadside buffets that serve up fried Nicaraguan dishes at night. If you turn north four blocks down the Calzada and walk a block towards Calle La Libertad you will find a *fritanga* that serves its food in plantain leaves. Around the corner is another. There is also a popular one next to Ciudad Lounge. *Fritangas* are not recommended for the weak-stomached, but it is interesting to go and see the different options.

Cafés

Café Sonrisa (from the Iglesia La Merced, 50 meters towards the Parque Colón, tel. 505/8376-4881, Mon.-Sat. 7am-3:30pm, $1-9) is staffed completely by deaf Nicaraguan youth. This project was born not only to create employment for these youth, but also to give voice to a population that is so often ignored by hearing people. The menu is designed to help facilitate communication between waiters and customers. Many local venders and neighborhood folks have become regulars, picking up a great deal of the sign language

Sign language tips accompany the menu at Café Sonrisa.

posted all around. This is a great place to use Wi-Fi, lounge in the biggest hammock you have ever seen, or try your hand at hammock-making in the workshop next door, where at-risk youth weave hammocks for sale.

Espressionista (Calle Xalteva, across the street from the southern side of the Xalteva Church, tel. 505/2552-4325, Wed.-Sun. 11am-10pm) is a new trendy café that has put its efforts into demonstrating that Nicaragua produces high-quality products. You can enjoy top-notch Nicaraguan coffee along with one of their imaginative baked goods, like calala (passion fruit) cheesecake. They also serve artisanal beer made by a German who lives a few cities over, have a constantly rotating menu of food, and make their own ice cream. (Try the rose flavor that comes from Matagalpa roses!)

Garden Cafe (Calle la Libertad, 1 block east of Parque Colón, tel. 505/2552-8582, gardencafegranada.com, daily 7am-9pm, $2-12) is a wonderful respite from the heat, with a cool space to enjoy great breakfasts, gourmet sandwiches, salads, smoothies, and coffee drinks. The artsy patio is a great place to crank the Wi-Fi. **Kathy's Waffle House** (across from Convento San Francisco, daily 7am-2pm, $5-8) is the closest thing to a U.S.-style diner, minus its breezy outdoor patio, serving up delicious pancakes, biscuits and gravy, eggs and bacon, and omelets. The colorful space of **Café de los Sueños** (on La Calzada 3.5 blocks from the cathedral, tel. 505/8324-2913, $4-12) is a great place to get in Wi-Fi time while you enjoy tasty sandwiches and artwork that will make you smile.

Upscale and International
★ **El Tercer Ojo** (Calle El Arsenal across from Convento San Francisco, tel. 505/2552-6451, Tues.-Sun. 11am-11pm, $7-20) offers everything from Spanish tapas and sushi to Gorgonzola pasta, kebabs, and fine wine in a gauzy lounge of candles and soothing music.

For lip-smacking, upscale Nicaraguan dishes and steaks, don't miss ★ **El Zaquan**

(behind the cathedral, daily noon-11pm, $15-25). Your nose should lead you to the meat-draped open-flame grill and dishes like *churrasco jalapeño.*

Pita Pita (Calle Libertad, 1 block from the central plaza, tel. 505/5758-3870, www.depitapita.com, $4-10) is an authentic Middle Eastern restaurant that serves hummus with tahini imported from Lebanon, shawarma sandwiches, and other Mediterranean and Middle Eastern dishes. The food is very fresh—the owner has an organic farm where he grows the vegetables used in the restaurant.

For highly recommended vegetarian food try ★ **El Garaje** (512 Calle Corral, from Convento San Francisco 2.25 blocks towards the lake, tel. 505/8651-7412, Mon.-Fri. 11:30am-6:30pm, $3-10) or **El Kapayuo** (Calle El Martirio, 2 blocks north of the Eskimo on La Calzada, Tues.-Sun., $4-20). Both have slightly odd hours and might take a little asking around to find but are well worth it for their healthy vegetarian meals.

For fresh Middle Eastern food, **Camello** (Calle el Caimito, 2 blocks towards the lake from the central plaza, tel. 505/2557-7546, dinner daily, lunch only during high season, $5-10) serves falafel and shawarma as well as curry dishes and other international food.

Ciudad Lounge (Calle la Libertad, 5 blocks west of Parque Colón, tel. 505/2552-1543, Thurs.-Sun. 6pm-midnight, $10-35) is probably the swankiest place in town, with a quality wine list, martinis, cacao liquor, a daily changing menu of international foods, and cigars from Estelí.

Charly's Bar (from Petronic, 5 blocks west and 25 meters south, tel. 505/2552-2942, Wed.-Mon. 11am-11pm, $4-10) is an all-time schnitzel-flinging favorite on the western fringes of town, specializing in German cuisine, BBQ, and draft beer in a huge crystal cowboy boot. It's far from the center of town, but worth the taxi ride.

Locals and backpackers rave about the prices at **Telepizza** (Calle La Calzada, 2 blocks from the Parque Colón, tel. 505/2552-4219, daily 10am-10pm, large pies from $6, delivery available). The gigantic stuffed calzones may be one of the best deals in town. You'll find authentic pizza at Monna Lisa (Calle La Calzada, tel. 505/2552-8187, $5-12). Get real, thin-crust Italian pizza baked in a wood-fire oven at Don Luca's (Calle La Calzada, tel. 505/2552-7822, $6-12).

INFORMATION AND SERVICES

Banks

Banco de America Central (BAC) is on the southwest corner of the central plaza. Banpro and Bancentro are on Calle Atravesada, just a few blocks away. The sanctioned moneychangers are out in full force along this same section of Atravesada (they're on the street, waving wads of cash). You'll find ATMs in most banks and at the Esso gas station on the edge of town.

Emergency Services

The police presence is pretty serious in Granada. You'll note an officer stationed full-time in Parque Colón, and a lot of others patrolling to keep tourists safe. If you are a victim of crime, you can file a report by email (webdenunciagr@policia.gob.ni) or visit the police station (tel. 505/2552-4712) on the highway to Nandaime or the one 75 meters west of the cinema (tel. 505/2552-2977 or 505/2552-2929). The regional Hospital Bernardino Díaz Ochoa (on road to Managua), the biggest hospital in the area, is a few kilometers out of town. A private option closer to town is the Hospital Privado Cocibolca (on road to Managua, tel. 505/2552-2907 or 505/2552-4092). For minor treatments, the section of Calle Atravesada just south of the bridge is occupied by more than a dozen clinics, blood labs, and pharmacies.

Tour Operators

Most of the national tour operators listed in the Essentials chapter have offices in Granada

that provide local trips and transfers. In addition, here are a few Granada specialists:

Leo Tours (tel. 505/8842-7905, leotoursgranada@gmail.com, leonica1971@yahoo.com), run by Leopoldo Castillo, a Granada native, incorporates a community-minded spirit that will connect you to Nicaragua rather than just show you the sights. They can take you around Granada, Ometepe, Laguna de Apoyo, and Mombacho, or show by bike tour how the "rest" of Granada lives.

Café Las Flores-Mombotour (cafelasflores.com, from $30 pp) offers several different canopy tours, including their popular Tarzan Swing. They will pick you up, and you can be out the door of your hotel and on belay in 30 minutes. They offer a plethora of other tours including their specialty coffee tour.

Tierra Tours (Calle La Calzada, 2 blocks east of Parque Colón, tel. 505/8862-9580, www.tierratours.com, $55 pp for full-service camping trip) offers trips to Mombacho, Masaya, and through Las Isletas, where they can coordinate kayak tours as well. They are also gaining traction as the go-to place for travelers—usually Spanish language students—looking for long-term homestays. In addition to local tours of Granada, Masaya, and Catarina, Tierra offers night tours of Volcán Masaya and overnight cabins and tent platforms at a nearby Butterfly Reserve and coffee farm. Ask about shuttle service to other parts of Nicaragua, including León, where they have a sister office.

Amigo Tours (tel. 505/2552-4080, www.amigotours.net, bernal@amigotours.net), connected to the lobby of the Hotel Colonial, provides a higher-end option for tours, plus travel agency services like national airline bookings, car rentals, and transfers to and from Costa Rica.

GETTING THERE AND AWAY

In addition to the options that follow, most tour operators listed in this chapter offer exclusive shuttles to and from San Juan del Sur, León, the dock for Ometepe, and the airport.

Bus

TO OTHER POINTS IN NICARAGUA

The easiest and most popular way to get here from Managua (or Masaya, which is on the way) is to grab a COGRAN *expreso* (1.5 blocks south of the central plaza's southwest corner, tel. 505/2552-2954). These medium-size express buses leave every 15-20 minutes daily 4:30am-7pm. (They stop service earlier on Sundays.) Another fleet of minivans *(micros)* leaves from Parque Sandino on the north side of Granada near the old railroad station, a few blocks from Parque Colón, with regular departures daily 5am-7:30pm. Both services leave from the UCA in Managua. From Granada, the same vehicles leave every 15 minutes daily 5:50am-8pm. If you don't mind not having a seat, you can catch either *micro* along Carretera Masaya. Note that the last bus of the day in either direction is usually the most packed.

Regular bus service from Rivas, Nandaime, and Jinotepe arrives to the Shell Palmira, on Granada's south side, just past the Palí supermarket. Buses to Rivas (1.5 hours) leave sporadically between 5:45am-3:10pm. Nandaime buses leave every 20 minutes. Jinotepe *expresos* take a mere 45 minutes compared to the nearly two-hour *ordinario* trip through the pueblos. Around the corner, behind the Palí, is the bus terminal with service to Masaya's city center (although any Managua-bound *expresos* will let you off along the highway through Masaya). Upon arrival at any of these locations, it's easiest to take a taxi to your hotel or Parque Colón; expect to pay about $1 per person.

TO COSTA RICA AND PANAMÁ

Avenida Arrellano, on the west end of Granada, is part of the San José and Panama City-bound routes for Central American bus lines. The two offices are located on the east side of the street. Reservations should be made at least two days in advance. For the Tica Bus terminal (half a block south of the Old Hospital, tel. 505/2552-4301), arrive at 6:15am for the 7am bus. TransNica (3 long blocks south of the Old Hospital, on the corner of Calle Xalteva, tel. 505/2552-6619) has three daily south-bounders, departing 6:30am, 8am, and 11am; be there a half-hour before departure. You should take a taxi ($0.50 pp) farther into town.

Boat

TO OMETEPE AND SAN CARLOS

Though the San Jorge ferry in Rivas is much more comfortable and direct way to get to Ometepe, it is possible to travel to Ometepe directly from Granada. Granada's crusty old ferry departs Granada's municipal dock (tel. 505/552-2966) Monday and Thursday at 2pm, arriving in San Carlos 6am. The price for a one-way passage between Granada and Ometepe is $10, but when lake is choppy, the ship will skip Ometepe altogether. The boat departs Granada on Mondays at 2pm (arriving in Altagracia, Ometepe around 6pm) and Thursdays at 3pm (arriving around 9pm). To get here from San Carlos, catch the ferry at 2pm, and from Ometepe, in Altagracia at midnight on Tuesdays and Fridays. It arrives at 4:30am on Wednesdays and Saturdays.

When weather permits, the boat stops at Altagracia before cutting across to the eastern lakeshore and port calls in Morrito and San Miguelito. The boat can get crowded and uncomfortable, especially around Semana Santa when the lake turns *bravo* (rough) and the weather is hot. Get to the port early and be aggressive to stake your territory.

A new option, the Barco Turístico ($20 first class, includes coffee and drink service; $13 economy), leaves Granada Fridays at 7pm, stopping only in Altagracia, then arriving in San Carlos the following morning at 6am. It departs San Carlos Sunday evening at 6pm. For more info, contact La Empresa Portuaria (tel. 505/2583-0256).

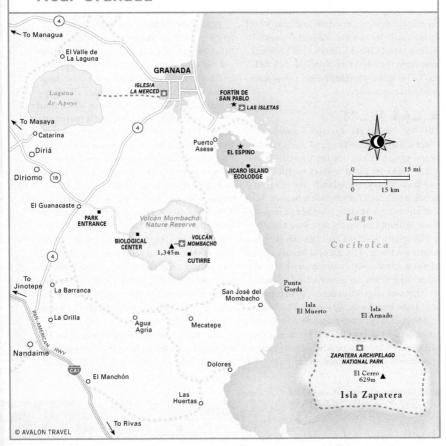

Near Granada

Map labels: To Managua · El Valle de La Laguna · GRANADA · IGLESIA LA MERCED · FORTÍN DE SAN PABLO · LAS ISLETAS · Laguna de Apoyo · To Masaya · Catarina · Diriá · Puerto Asese · EL ESPINO · JICARO ISLAND ECOLODGE · Diriomo · El Guanacaste · PARK ENTRANCE · Volcán Mombacho Nature Reserve · Lago Cocibolca · BIOLOGICAL CENTER · VOLCÁN MOMBACHO · 1,345m · CUTIRRE · To Jinotepe · La Barranca · San José del Mombacho · Punta Gorda · La Orilla · Agua Agria · Mecatepe · Isla El Muerto · Isla El Armado · Nandaime · Dolores · ZAPATERA ARCHIPELAGO NATIONAL PARK · El Manchón · El Cerro 629m · Isla Zapatera · Las Huertas · To Rivas · © AVALON TRAVEL · 0 15 mi · 0 15 km

GETTING AROUND

Most of the top sights lie in the kilometer between the lake and the plaza, and they are all walkable. Walking is the best way to enjoy the city, and it's best to walk in the early morning when the temperature is still pleasant. You can also explore Granada's narrow streets via horse and carriage ($10-15/hour). Find the carriages along the western, shady side of the plaza. Please patronize only those drivers who seem to be taking good care of their animals. Though the situation is improving, the occasional bag-o-bones with open saddle sores are still around. The pleasant tour will help orient you for the rest of your stay. Taxis are numerous and cheap (less than $1).

Car Rental

The Budget office (in the Shell Guapinol gas station on the road to Managua, tel. 505/2552-2323, reserve@budget.com.ni, daily 8am-6:30pm, car rental $30-110/day) rents cars and cell phones. There is huge demand for their 28-vehicle fleet, so reservations are necessary, especially in the high season. Hotels also often maintain a list of trusted cars and drivers, and many tour operators have extra vehicles. For car rentals, drivers, transfers, and four-wheel drive, call Peter van der Meijs at **Armadillo Nicaragua** (4 blocks north and 1.5 blocks west from the Shell Guapinol, tel. 505/8833-8663, armadillo-nicaragua.com, info@arma-dillo-nicaragua.com).

★ LAS ISLETAS

This 365-island archipelago formed when Volcán Mombacho erupted some 20,000 years ago, hurling its top half into the nearby lake in giant masses of rock, ash, and lava. Today, the islands are inhabited by a few hundred *campesinos* (country folk) and an ever-increasing number of wealthy Nicaraguans and foreigners who continue to buy up the *isletas* to build garish vacation homes on them. The natural beauty of the *isletas* is spectacular, and history buffs will enjoy the **Fortín de San Pablo,** a Spanish fort that was largely unsuccessful in preventing pirate attacks on Granada. The islanders themselves are interesting and friendly, maintaining a rural lifestyle unique in Nicaragua: Children paddle dugout canoes or rowboats to school from an early age, and

their parents get along by fishing and farming or by taking camera-toting tourists for a ride in their boats.

Almost every hotel and tour operator offers a trip to Las Isletas and may pair it with other excursions. There are a *lot* of options out there. For example, the Mombotour office in Granada offers an introductory three-hour kayak class ($34), which includes all equipment, sea kayaks, transportation, and a tour of the Fortín de San Pablo. For a more economical option, go right to the boat owners at the Marina Cocibolca. If you take a taxi to the southern end of the waterfront road there are many *lancheros* (boat drivers). Don't expect to haggle over prices, as gasoline is expensive (see for yourself at the dockside station). You'll pay about $10 per person for a half-hour tour, more for longer or farther trips. You can take a dip in the lake water or have your *lanchero* bring you to the cemetery, old fort, or **monkey island,** which is inhabited by a community of monkeys. If you want to eat lunch, ask your guide if you can stop at one of island restaurants or visit a local family who can serve you lunch.

There are a couple of upscale options for staying on one of the islands. The swankiest is **Jicaro Island Lodge** (tel. 505/2558-7702,

Rent a kayak to enjoy the natural beauty of Las Isletas.

Monkeys populate many of the *isletas*.

toucans, herons, and other waterfowl, plus white-tailed deer and an alleged population of jaguars no one ever seems to see.

These islands were enormously important to the Nahuatl, who used them primarily as a vast burial ground and sacrifice spot. The sites of La Punta de las Figuras and Zonzapote are particularly rich in artifacts and have a network of caves that have never been researched. Seek out the petroglyphs carved into the bedrock beaches of Isla el Muerto. An impressive selection of Zapatera's formidable stone idols is on display in the Convento San Francisco, but the islands' remaining archaeological treasures remain relatively unstudied and unprotected and (naturally) continue to disappear.

Officially declared a national park by the Sandinistas in 1983, the Zapatera Archipelago has never been adequately protected or funded. MARENA's thousand-page management plan document is just that—a document—while in reality, only one park ranger visits the islands a couple of times per month. It's no surprise then that inhabitants and visitors litter, loot the archaeological patrimony, hunt, and cut down trees for timber.

Visiting Zapatera

Access the islands from Granada's Puerto Asese, where you can strike a deal with returning Zapatera islanders or hire a tourist boat. The most reliable way is to arrange a trip with Zapatera Tours (tel. 505/8842-2587, www.zapateratours.com), a small company that specializes in creative lake tours, including overnight camping trips, fishing, and waterskiing. You can also inquire about Zapatera trips with any of the other Granada tour companies. With a fast, powerful motor, it's a 20-minute trip from Granada, partly over a stretch of open water that can get choppy.

There are a scattering of places to stay around the island, including a cheap dormitory and homestay options in Zonzapote. Or book a room at Casa Hacienda Hotel Santa María (tel. 505/8884-0606,

www.jicarolodge.com, $560 d, includes 3 meals a day), where you can watch the sun sink over the water from a beautiful two-story *casita* (cottage). A newer option with an up-close view of Mombacho is El Espino (tel. 505/7636-0060, www.isletaelespino.com, $120-195 d, includes transport and breakfast). The solar-powered lodge features a swimming pool, yoga platform, and massage facilities. They gladly accept day-trippers, call ahead for prices.

★ ZAPATERA ARCHIPELAGO NATIONAL PARK

About 34 kilometers south of Granada, Zapatera is an extinct volcano surrounded by Isla el Muerto and a dozen or so other islets, all of which comprise 45 square kilometers of land; the whole complex is home for some 500 residents. Zapatera is a natural wonder, rising 629 meters above sea level. Its virgin forest is rife with myriad wildlife such as parrots, santamariaislazapatera@gmail.com, $50 pp day use, $120 d, plus meals, transport, and fishing trips), where the Cordova family's 120-year-old tile-roofed ranch house has been outfitted with comfortably primitive double rooms with mosquito net, fan, and private bathrooms. The hotel is on a relaxing sandy beach, looking north toward Isla el Muerto and Mombacho.

★ VOLCÁN MOMBACHO

Mombacho is unavoidable. It towers over the southern horizon, lurks around every corner, creeps into your panoramic photos. In Granada, you are living in the shadow of a (fortunately gentle) giant. Every bit of cool, misty, cloud forest higher than 850 meters above sea level is officially protected as a nature reserve (tel. 505/2552-5858, entrance fee: $20 foreigners, $8 Nicas and residents, $10 students and children). This equals about 700 hectares of park, rising to a peak elevation of 1,345 meters, and comprising a rich, concentrated island of flora and fauna. Thanks to the Fundación Cocibolca, the reserve is accessible and makes available the best-designed and maintained hiking trails in the nation.

Overgrown with hundreds of orchid and bromeliad species, tree ferns, and old-growth cloud and dwarf forests, Mombacho also boasts three species of monkeys, 168 observed birds (49 of which are migratory), 30 species of reptiles, 60 mammals (including at least one very secretive big cat), and 10 amphibians. The flanks of the volcano, 21 percent of which remains forested, are composed of privately owned coffee plantations and cattle ranches. Maintaining the forest canopy is a crucial objective of Fundación Cocibolca, since this is where more than 90 percent of Mombacho's 1,000 howler monkeys reside (the monkeys travel in 100 different troops and venture into the actual reserve only to forage).

Although the majority of Mombacho's visitors arrive as part of a tour package, it is entirely possible to visit the reserve on your own, and it makes a perfect day trip from Managua, Granada, or Masaya. You'll start by taking a bus (or express minivan) headed for Nandaime or Rivas (or, from Granada, to Carazo as well); tell the driver to let you off at the Empalme el Guanacaste. This is a large intersection. The road up to the parking lot and official reserve entrance is located 1.5 kilometers toward the mountain—look for the signs. The walk to the parking lot is a solid half-hour trek, mostly uphill and in the sun. Water and snacks are available at the parking

the view from Volcán Mombacho

lot. Drink lots before and during this first leg of your journey. Once you arrive at the parking lot, you'll pay the entrance fee and then board one of the foundation's vehicles to make the half-hour, six-kilometer climb up to the Biological Station. The lumbering troop transports depart daily at 8:30am, 10am, and 1:30pm. The entrance fee includes admission to the reserve, transport to and from the top of the volcano, and insurance. If you've got the time, the shoes, and the strong legs, feel free to hike all the way up the steep road yourself. If you choose to walk, the cost reduces to $5 for foreign adults. Allow a couple of hours (and lots of water) to reach the top.

Trails

There is a short (half-hour) trail through the Café Las Flores coffee farm at the bottom of the volcano, where you wait for your ride up. Once on top, there are three trails to choose from: Sendero el Cráter, which encircles the forest-lined crater, and features a moss-lined tunnel, several lookouts, and a spur trail to the *fumaroles* (holes in the ground venting hot sulfurous air). The *fumaroles* area is an open, grassy part of the volcano with blazing wild-flowers and an incredible view of Granada and the *isletas*. The whole loop, including

the spur, is 1.5 kilometers, with a few ups and downs, and takes 1.5 hours to walk. The Sendero El Tigrillo ($4) is a breathtaking 2.5-hour hike. The Sendero la Puma ($6) is considerably more challenging and requires that you go with a guide. This four-kilometer loop with several difficult climbs that lead to breathtaking viewpoints begins at a turnoff from the *fumaroles* trail; allow a minimum of three hours to complete it (bring lots of water). Well-trained, knowledgeable local guides (some with English) are available for the Sendero el Cráter ($7 per group, plus tip), Sendero el Tigrillo ($10), and are required for Sendero la Puma ($15). Note, because of the altitude and the clouds, the visibility from these trails may be much diminished on bad-weather days.

Volcán Mombacho Biological Center

Located at the base of one of Mombacho's 14 communications antennas, on a small plateau called Plan de las Flores at 1,150 meters, the research station is also an interpretive center, *hospedaje, cafetín,* ranger station, and conference center, technically completed in 2000 but still expanding. Find drinks and snacks here, including simple meals. Currently,

A truck will take you six kilometers up to the Biological Station on top of Mombacho.

the *albergue* (hostel; $50 pp, includes dinner and breakfast) has 10 dormitory beds in a loft above the interpretive center. You can also pitch a tent ($20) and buy meals on the side. To make a reservation, contact the Biological Station (tel. 505/2248-8234/35 or 505/2552-5858); or contact Fundación Cocibolca (tel. 505/2278-3224 or 505/2277-1681, www.mombacho.org) in Managua. Most tour companies will get you there; start with Café Las Flores-Mombotour (cafelasflores.com) or Tierra Tours (505/8862-9580, www.tierratours.com).

Canopy Tours

Put yourself on belay at the Mombacho Canopy Tour (tel. 505/8888-2566 or 505/8852-9483, gloriamaria@cablenet.com.ni, $40), located up the road from the parking lot, just before the road passes through the El Progreso coffee mill. Their 1,500-meter course involves 15 platforms and a 25-meter-long hanging bridge. Many tour operators offer a full-day Mombacho package that involves a visit to the reserve followed by a canopy tour on the way down, or you can arrange it yourself by calling Fundación Cocibolca.

Masaya

Masaya sprawls over a tropical plain nestled against the slopes of the volcano by the same name; at its western edge, paths carved by the Chorotega people trace the steep hillside down to the Laguna de Masaya. Twenty indigenous villages of Darianes used to cluster at the water's edge. Masaya was officially founded as a city in 1819 and has grown ever since. Several centuries of rebellion and uprising—first against the Spaniards in 1529 and later against William Walker's forces in 1856, the U.S. Marines in 1912, and a number of ferocious battles against the National Guard during the revolution—earned the Masayans a reputation as fierce fighters.

Travelers find Masaya less polished than Granada, and it's true that the streets and building facades in Masaya are less cared for. But Masayans are a creative people with many traditions found nowhere else in Nicaragua, such as their solemn, mysterious funeral processions. Your best introduction to these delights is Masaya's Mercado Viejo (Old Market), which is so pleasant and compelling that many visitors choose not to stray beyond its stately stone walls. But it's worth exploring further to people-watch in the central park and make your way over to the breezy *malecón* for the impressive views of the Laguna de Masaya 100 meters below.

ORIENTATION

Masaya sits due south of the Managua-Granada highway along the east side of the Laguna de Masaya. The street that runs north along the central plaza's east side is Calle Central. As you travel along it toward the highway, it becomes increasingly commercial. One block east of the southeast corner of the central plaza, you'll find the stone facade of the Mercado Viejo (Old Market). Six blocks west of the central plaza are the hammock factories, baseball stadium, and *malecón;* three blocks north are a handful of budget hostel options. Traveling due south leads to Barrio Monimbó. Going five blocks north puts you in the heart of the Barrio San Jerónimo around the church of the same name, situated at the famous *siete esquinas* (seven corners) intersection. The heart of Masaya is easily walkable, but one of the city's several hundred taxis (less than $1) or a public bus are recommended to get to the *malecón* or the highway.

SIGHTS

Masaya's central plaza is officially called Parque 17 de Octubre, named for a battle against Somoza's Guardia in 1977. Plenty of remaining bullet holes are testimony, plus two imposing command towers immediately to the west. It is a common meeting place for

Masaya

EL MALECÓN

COCO JAMBO
OLD HOSPITAL
ESTADIO ROBERTO CLEMENTE
HAMMOCK WORKSHOPS

CARRETERA MASAYA

To Managua
★ COYOTEPE

MAP AREA
CALLE CENTRAL

OLD TRAIN STATION
ZONA ALFS
FRITANGA CHEPA RATONA

To Tipitapa

CALLE MONIMBÓ

Monimbó

BUS TERMINAL
NEW MARKET
HOTEL ROSALYN'S

To Granada

To Catarina

0   100 yds
0   100 m

Parque San Juan
IGLESIA SAN JUAN

CENTRO DE CULTURA
MUSEO Y GALERÍA HÉROES Y MÁRTIRES

IGLESIA SAN JERÓNIMO

CLARO
BANCENTRO
PALI

HOTEL CASA ROBLETO

HOSTAL MI CASA
MADERA'S INN HOTEL

LIBRARY

LA PARROQUIA LA ASUNCIÓN
Parque 17 de Octubre

LA RONDA
INTERNET

CALLE MONIMBÓ

To Plaza Monimbó

BDF

CEVICHES EL POLLO
KAFFE CAFÉ

JAROCHITA'S
POLICE

CALLE CENTRAL

BANK

UNO

CALLE EL CALVARIO

To Old Train Station, Zona Alfs, and Fritanga Chepa Ratóna

BANPRO
NANI CAFÉ

EL MERCADO VIEJO/ CRAFT MARKET
CHE GRIS

LA EMILINA NATA

Parque San Miguel

To New Market and Bus Terminal

© AVALON TRAVEL

Masayans of all walks of life, and is great for people-watching (it also has free Wi-Fi). The church in the northeast corner is La Parroquia La Asunción.

The triangular Plaza de Monimbó park on the southern side of Masaya comes to life every afternoon at 4pm as the throbbing social and commercial heart of the mostly indigenous Monimbó neighborhood. Climb the Iglesia San Jerónimo church four blocks north of the central plaza to get a great view of the city and its surroundings. Ask permission from one of the guards before heading up.

The Museo y Galería Héroes y Mártires (inside the Alcaldía, 1.5 blocks north of the central plaza, Mon.-Fri. 8am-5pm, donation requested) pays tribute to those Masayans who fought Somoza's National Guard during the revolution with a collection of guns and photos of the fallen. The highlight is the unexploded napalm bomb Somoza dropped on the city in 1977.

El Mercado Viejo

★ El Mercado Viejo Craft Market

All roads lead to El Mercado Viejo, built in 1891, destroyed by fires in 1966 and 1978, and refurbished in 1997 as a showcase for local handicrafts. Also known as El Mercado Nacional de Artesanías, or simply the "tourist market," El Mercado Viejo is safe, comfortable, and geared toward foreigners. You'll find all manner of delightful surprises: locally made leather shoes, brass, iron, carved wood, and textile handicrafts, plus paintings, clothing and hammocks. This is the best of what Nicaragua's talented craftspeople have to offer and it's the best reason to come to Masaya. Even if you don't buy anything, the market is an enjoyable and colorful experience. Of course, you pay for the convenience in slightly higher prices.

El Malecón

Cool off after an intense morning in the market on the windswept *malecón,* a beautiful cliffside promenade with long views over the Volcán Masaya crater lake to the north and west. Set at the foot of the volcano, the Laguna de Masaya is 8.5 square kilometers and 73 meters deep in the center. It's also one of the country's most polluted lakes. While several trails, some of which were made by the Chorotegas themselves, lead the intrepid hiker down to the water's edge, this is no swimming hole. Dip your heels in nearby Laguna de Apoyo instead. The view is beautiful but the area is known for higher levels of common crime, so be extra vigilant with cameras and valuables. It's easily reached from the city center.

Artisan Workshops

Nicaragua's most treasured souvenirs, woven hammocks, are handmade by scores of Masaya families, taking 2-3 days each to make. The most obvious place to purchase one is in one of Masaya's public markets. More fun than simply buying a hammock, visit one of the many *fábricas de hamacas* (across from the old hospital on the road to the *malecón* and baseball stadium), most of which are in people's homes, clustered on the same block near the southwest edge of town. There you'll find at least a half-dozen family porch-front businesses; all of these craftspeople will gladly show you how hammocks are woven.

Sergio Zepeda is a third-generation luthier (maker of stringed instruments) at Guitarras Zepeda (200 meters west of the Unión Fenosa, tel. 505/8883-0260, guitarraszepeda@yahoo.com). His shop is only a block off Carretera Masaya, behind Hotel Rosalyn. Cheap children's and beater guitars start at $60; professional hardwood instruments with cocobolo rosewood back and sides, and imported red cedar, mahogany, or spruce tops can go for up to $800. Allow at least two weeks to order, or show up in his shop and see what's available.

ENTERTAINMENT AND EVENTS

Check out Jueves de Verbena (Mercado Viejo, Thurs. 5pm-11pm), which consists of dance, theater, art expos, music, and more, all presented in the Old Market on one of several stages. Rub elbows with the locals at the most popular local bar in town, La Ronda (south side of the central plaza), with beer, lots of space, and good appetizers. Kaffé

Café Bistro (western part of the central plaza, tel. 505/2522-2200) also often has live music on Saturday evenings; check their Facebook page for listings. Zona Alf's (behind the old train station, tel. 505/8981-5017) and Coco Jambo (by the *malecón*) are popular places to go dancing; take a taxi to the *malecón* at night instead of walking.

If you're here on a weekend during baseball season (Nov.-May), be sure to catch the local team, San Fernando, which plays in Estadio Roberto Clemente (on the malecón, from $0.50), named for the Puerto Rico-born Pittsburgh Pirate who died in a plane crash in 1973 delivering relief aid to Nicaraguan earthquake victims. The tailgating scene atop the *malecón* may be one of the most scenic in the world.

ACCOMMODATIONS

Along the highway and outside of town, Masaya's hotels tend to be pay-by-the-hour *auto-hotels*. These are mainly used for romantic escapades (nifty car park curtains hide license plates from spying eyes). In town, lodging is reasonable but not nearly as varied or polished as Granada.

Just a few blocks north of the central plaza there are a handful of small reasonably

Handwoven hammocks take 2-3 days each to make.

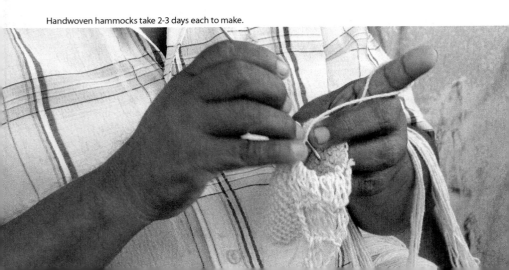

Masaya's Fiestas

Masayans celebrate all year long, observing various religious, historical, and indigenous rites with a wild collage of marimba music, traditional costume, poetry, painting, food, drink, and age-old customs. Costumes are a key element of the festivals and are often elaborate and gorgeous.

A few weeks before Easter, the celebration of San Lázaro features believers promenading with their ornately costumed dogs to thank their patron saint for keeping their household animals in good health.

In the Festival of the Cross, celebrated in May, in honor of La Señora de la Asunción, people exchange thousands of palm-thatch crosses to remember the miracle that occurred during the last eruption of Volcán Masaya's Santiago Crater, in which the virgin saved the city from hot ashes.

September through December are peak fiesta months in Masaya. Things get started with the official *fiestas patronales* (Sept. 20) in honor of Patron Saint Jerónimo. On the penultimate Friday of October, the Fiesta de los Agüisotes (Fiesta of Bad Omens) is a nod to Nicaragua's darker side: Folks dress up as scary figures from local legends, such as the *chancha bruja* (pig witch) and the *mocuana* (a woman who haunts La Mocuana Hill). This is a huge party night in the city and young people come from far and wide to dress up and go to the various parties around town, including a huge concert in the Old Market. The Fiesta del Toro Venado, on the last Sunday of October, is similar to Agüisotes, but it happens during the day. Masayans don disguises that poke fun at their favorite politicians, clergy, and other public figures.

Patron-saint celebrations end the first Sunday of December with the Procesión de San Jerónimo. This is perhaps the most stunning of Masaya's fiestas, as the statue of the city's patron saint is paraded through the streets amidst a sea of flowers. Every Sunday September-December features a folk dance of some sort, a competition between rival troops, or even dancers that go from house to house performing short dances to marimba music.

In mid-January, the Festival of San Sebastian explodes with life and energy in the indigenous Monimbó barrio. The celebration's highlight is the Baile de Chinegro de Mozote y Verga, in which participants engage in a mock battle, hitting each other with big sticks and finally coming together in a peace ritual.

Pieces and parcels of Masaya's festivals are found in the various *fiestas patronales* of the many surrounding pueblos, each of which present their own peculiar twist to the events. In mid-June, for example, San Juan de Oriente's party involves "warriors" dancing through the streets and whipping each other with stiffened bull penises.

priced hostels. ★ Madera's Inn Hotel (2 blocks south of the fire station, tel. 505/2522-5825, maderasinn.com, maderasinn@yahoo.com, $6 dorm, $15-45 private) is the nicest of the bunch; its 12 rooms occupy two floors set around a pleasant common room. You'll find friendly service, Internet access, parking, airport shuttle, tours, and laundry service. Some rooms have a fan and shared bath; more expensive rooms have private baths and air-conditioning.

One block towards the plaza there are four more budget hostels. Hostal Mi Casa (behind Fruti-Fruti smoothie bar and *cafetín*, tel. 505/2522-2500, $7-10 pp) has an open, colorful common space.

Found in an old colonial home near the church, ★ Hotel Casa Robleto (1.5 blocks south of Parque San Jerónimo, there is no sign so ask around, tel. 505/2522-2617, casarobleto@hotmail.com, $50 d, includes breakfast) is a well-run elegant bed-and-breakfast. The house is beautifully furnished with antique wooden furniture, like a locally made wooden chess set. The rooms have air-conditioning, Wi-Fi, and hot water.

FOOD
Fritanga and Local Fare

For authentic street food, visit Masaya's Plaza de Monimbó (across from the Don Bosco school, daily from 4pm). Vendors set up in the small triangular plaza. You'll find everything from standard finger-licking *fritanga* served on a banana leaf to hard-core snout-to-tail pig dishes and organ meat, such as that featured on the Travel Channel's *Bizarre Foods with Andrew Zimmern* "Nicaragua" episode.

Countless small *comedores* (cheap lunch counters) line both sides of the main street from the central plaza all the way up to the old train station. You'll find juicy, greasy, fried, and roasted treasures at one of several locally famous street grills: Fritanga San Jerónimo (a few blocks west of the church with the same name); La Emilina Ñata en el Barrio Loco (daily from 5pm), or Flat-nose Emilina's in the Crazy Neighborhood, open 'til its world-famous grilled beef runs out. After a late night party, Fritanga La Chepa Ratona (next to the old train station) is a popular option.

Cafés and Restaurants

Masaya has a burgeoning restaurant scene with a handful of new cafés and upscale restaurants. ★ Kaffé Café (across the street from the western edge of the central plaza, tel. 505/7725-2200, www.kaffecafebistro.com, $4-14) is a fine restaurant and café that serves elegant food, like delicious panini and toasted wraps. Vegetarians, don't miss the stuffed pepper with hummus. They also brew quality coffee, have a good selection of local and international beers, and often have live music on Saturday evenings. Nani Café (across the street from the south side of Mercado Viejo, tel. 505/2522-3909, lananicafe.com, $2-7) is a great place to cool off with air-conditioning and eat a quality Nicaraguan meal, or enjoy a pastry and cappuccino (complete with foam drawing). Che Gris (on east side of Mercado Viejo, tel. 505/2522-0394, www.restaurantechegris.com, $7-10) is an upscale bar and grill that offers traditional cooking in an air-conditioned setting. A lively, popular option is Jarochita's (north of the central plaza, tel. 505/2522-4831, daily 11am-10pm, $3-8), preparing Mexican cuisine with a Nicaraguan twist.

The iconic ★ Ceviches el Pollo (on western edge of the central plaza, tel. 505/8899-2776, www.cevicheselpollomasaya.com, $2-15) is known for its sky-high wooden tables and wide selection of fruit smoothies. Pick from 72 different smoothie combinations or order a fresh seafood ceviche. One of the waiters or, more likely, the owner himself, will bring it up to easily 10 feet in the air.

Ceviches el Pollo

Fried Food Galore: Eating at *Fritangas*

fried foods typically found at the *fritanga*

For most Nicaraguans, the *fritanga* is a place in the neighborhood to buy prepared food for dinner. Nearly every neighborhood has at least one *fritanga:* a grill and maybe a few tables set up in front of someone's house where they sell food buffet-style and usually to-go. Most food at the *fritanga* is made just as it sounds: *frito* (fried). It's not recommended for the weak-stomached traveler, but it is worth taking a peek to get an idea of typical foods. The following terms will help you navigate:

carne asado: grilled beef
chancho (cerdo): grilled pork
enchiladas: Nicaraguan enchiladas are two tortillas filled with rice and shredded beef, folded in half, and deep-fried. Served with cabbage salad, ketchup, and crema (similar to mayonnaise).
gallo pinto: "Speckled Rooster" is rice and beans fried together with onion and sometimes green pepper or carrot.
maduro: fried ripe plantain, mashed and fried into a ball with a chunk of cheese in the middle
pollo asado: grilled chicken
repocheta: deep fried tortilla topped with refried beans, crumbled salty cheese, cabbage salad, and usually ketchup and crema
res: fried meat patty, basically a hamburger
tacos: Unlike Mexican tacos, Nicaraguan tacos are tortillas filled with shredded meat, rolled up, and deep-fried. Served as a side or with cabbage salad, ketchup, and crema (similar to mayonnaise). You can ask for them without condiments if you prefer.
tajadas: green plantain chips served as a side or with cabbage salad and a piece of fried cheese
torta de papa: mashed potatoes, with a chunk of cheese in the middle, fried into a ball

INFORMATION AND SERVICES

Hospital Hilario Sanchez Vásquez (on the highway toward Granada, tel. 505/2522-2778) is the biggest facility in town, though you are much better off driving to **Hospital Vivan Pellas** (on the highway before you reach Managua). The large, blue **police station** (half a block north of Mercado Viejo, tel. 505/2522-4222 or 505/2522-2521) is across from Norma's bakery. Besides the multiple **ATMs** within the Mercado Viejo, numerous banks are close by: Bancentro (on the west side of the central plaza) and a BDF (one block north of Mercado Viejo).

GETTING THERE AND AWAY

Nearly every southbound bus leaving Managua from Roberto Huembes passes Masaya, which is right on the highway, only 27 kilometers from Managua. Faster still are the Masaya- or Granada-bound *expresos* from the UCA leaving regularly 6am-7:30pm daily, arriving half a block north of Masaya's Parque San Miguel; from there, they depart for Managua 6am-8pm daily. The ride costs under $1. There is also *expreso* service between Masaya's Plaza de Monimbó and Mercado Oriental in Managua, 3am-7pm daily. Ordinary bus service leaves and arrives at the main terminal in the parking lot of the Mercado Nuevo. From any point of arrival, you can take a taxi to the center for less than $1.

Buses bound for Granada leave 6am-7pm daily from the UCA terminal in Managua, stopping along the highway in Masaya en route. You can catch one of these *micros* from the gas station on the highway in Masaya to get to Granada. To get here from Granada, hop any Managua-bound bus.

★ VOLCÁN MASAYA NATIONAL PARK

An extraordinary and easy day trip from Managua, Masaya, or Granada, Volcán Masaya National Park (tel. 505/2528-1444, daily 9am-4:45pm, $4) is Nicaragua's most impressive outdoor attraction and premier tourist site. There are very few volcanoes in the world where you can simply drive up to the crater edge and look into what the Spaniards declared to be the "mouth of hell." Masaya offers exactly this, and more. One of the most visibly active volcanoes in the country, Volcán Masaya emits a nearly constant plume of sulfurous gas, smoke, and sometimes ash, visible from as far away as the airport in Managua. From one of its craters, you can sometimes glimpse incandescent rock and magma. A visitor's center (where you'll be asked to park your car facing out "just in case") will help you interpret the geology and ecology of the site, as will the park's impressive nature museum. For the more actively inclined, hiking trails cover a portion of the volcano's slopes.

Volcán Masaya was called Popogatepe (mountain that burns) by the Chorotegas, who interpreted eruptions as displays of anger to be appeased with sacrifices, often human. In the early 1500s, Father Francisco Bobadilla

buses headed for Masaya

Near Masaya

To Managua

Ticuantepe

To Tipitapa

Nindirí   COYOTEPE

El Crucero   Volcán
Masaya   EL MERCADO VIEJO
CRAFT MARKET
MASAYA

76

VOLCÁN MASAYA
NATIONAL PARK   Laguna
de Masaya

To
Granada

MARIPOSA ECO-HOTEL
& SPANISH SCHOOL

La Concepción   Nandasmo   CATARINA
MIRADOR   El Valle de La
Laguna

San
Marcos   Masatepe   Catarina   LAGUNA
DE APOYO

Pio XII   Diriá

San Diego

Citalapa

San
Cayetano

Santo
Domingo   San Rafael
del Sur

Niquinohomo   SAN JUAN
DE ORIENTE   Diriomo

Diriamba   El
Guanacaste

Jinotepe   Volcán
Mombacho
1,345m

Santa
Teresa   PAN-AMERICAN HWY

Masachapa

La Union

Nandaime

Pochomil   Tecolapa

La Conquista

La Trinidad   Casares   Ochomogo

La Boquita

Casares

CARAZO
BEACHES   Huehuete   Escalante   To
Rivas

PACIFIC
OCEAN   Escalante

Chacocente

0   5 mi

0   5 km   El Astillero   To
Tola   Nagualapa

© AVALON TRAVEL

placed a cross at the crater lip in order to exorcise the devil within and protect the villages below. Not long afterward, though, thinking the volcano might contain gold instead of the devil, both Friar Blas del Castillo and Gonzalo Fernandez de Oviedo lowered themselves into the crater on ropes. They found neither the devil nor gold and probably singed their eyebrows.

The park is composed of several geologically linked volcanic craters: **Volcán Nindirí,** which last erupted in 1670, and **Volcán Masaya,** which blew its top in 1772. The relatively new **Santiago Crater** was formed between the other two in 1852, and is inhabited by a remarkable species of parakeet that nests contentedly in the rocky side of the crater walls, oblivious to the toxic gases and the scientists who had thought such a sulphurous environment would be uninhabitable. You might see these *chocoyos del cráter* (crater parakeets) from the parking area along the crater's edge.

As for the sensation of "just in case," the danger is quite real. In April 2000, the Santiago crater burped up a single volcanic boulder that plummeted to earth, crushing an unfortunate Italian tourist's car in the parking lot. In April of 2012 the park closed temporarily due to the Santiago Crater's emission of incandescent material that caused a fire that spread across three acres.

Visiting Volcán Masaya

The exhibits at the Visitors Interpretation Center and museum include three-dimensional dioramas of Nicaragua and Central America, models of active volcanoes, and remnants of indigenous sacrifice urns and musical instruments found deep in the volcano's caves; there is also a display of old lithographs and paintings of the volcano as the Spaniards saw it. Consider one of several guided tours ($1-2 day tours, sign up at the visitors center), including an exciting night tour beginning at sunset ($10, call to reserve, minimum of 6 people). Of special interest is the walk to the Tzinancanostoc Bat Cave, a lava tube passageway melted out of solid rock.

Though most visitors only snap a few photos from the crater's edge before continuing on, the park contains several hiking trails through a veritable moonscape of lava formations and scrubby vegetation, making it easy to spend at least half a day here. Carry lots of water and sunscreen (there is little to

no shade). The worthwhile trails offer good opportunities to cross paths with some of the park's wildlife, including coyotes, deer, iguanas, and monkeys. The Coyote Trail will lead you east to the shore of the Laguna de Masaya.

Any Masaya- or Granada-bound bus from Managua (or Managua-bound bus from one of these cities) will drop you on the highway at the entrance to Volcán Masaya. If you have a car you can drive right up to the crater lip.

COYOTEPE

Just south of the volcano on a hill overlooking the highway, the battlements of fort Coyotepe (daily 8:30am-5pm, $2) overlook the city of Masaya. Take a cab or hike up the road. The view of Masaya, its lagoon, and the Masaya and Mombacho volcanoes, both great lakes, and the far-reaching surrounding countryside is worth it, and that's before you even descend into the dungeons. Built at the turn of the 20th century, this site witnessed a fierce battle between national troops and U.S. Marines in 1912. Somoza rehabilitated it as a particularly cruel prison. Today, Coyotepe is in the hands of the Nicaraguan Boy Scouts, who will accompany you through the pitch-black underground prison facilities in exchange for a small fee.

Volcán Masaya constantly emits sulfurous gas and ash.

NINDIRÍ

Just north of the highway between the entrance to the national park and the city of Masaya, Nindirí was the most important and densely populated of the indigenous settlements in the area up to 1,500 years before the arrival of the Spanish. Its name in Chorotega means Hill of the Small Pig, and its principal attraction is the 1,000-artifact collection in the **Museo Tenderí** (Mon-Fri. 8:30am-noon, tel. 505/8954-0570), named after a local cacique, which celebrates pre-Columbian culture. Ask around about the Cailagua site, with petroglyphs overlooking the Laguna de Masaya. Buses running between Managua, Masaya, and Granada will drop you off on the highway that runs along the edge of town. From there, you can take a taxi or walk a few blocks north to the center of town. Buses leaving from Masaya's Mercado Nuevo will take you direct into the city proper.

★ LAGUNA DE APOYO

Nicaragua's cleanest and most enticing swimming hole is the Laguna de Apoyo, just outside of Masaya. Actually a lagoon that formed in the drowned volcanic crater of the long extinct Volcán Apoyo, the lagoon floor reaches 200 meters in depth, the lowest point in all of Central America. Despite its continued seismicity—a minor earthquake in 2000 under the crater-rim town of Catarina caused Apoyo's water to slosh back and forth, wrecking a few homes—for the most part the volcano is considered dormant, and a thick green forest has grown up the slopes over the years. The valley of the lagoon is a national park and the slopes harbor a few hiking trails and are protected from further development by law. The crater hosts a few fish species found nowhere else on earth; scientists at the Proyecto Ecológico are studying them. If you hike through the forests, expect to observe species of toucan, hummingbirds, blue jays, howler and white-face monkeys (which are prone to fling their feces at you if you approach), and rare butterflies. There have been a few minor robberies over the years on the hiking paths, so carry as little of value as possible on a hike. There are few places on earth quite like this charming, isolated community.

Accommodations and Food

The number of places to eat or lodge along the western shore of the crater lake is continually improving, despite local grumbling about illegal development of the waterfront. At any establishment listed here, pay $5-10 to

The Laguna de Apoyo fills a long-extinct volcano.

stay for the day and enjoy the docks, kayaks, inner tubes, hammocks, and other facilities. The area has few stores or shops, and few services, so either pack your essentials before coming, or count on one of the local hotels or restaurants. Most hotels offer cheap shuttles from Granada, or you can hire a taxi or take a bus. All of the beachfront properties of the Laguna slope down towards the water and have lots of steps that require walking up and down to the waterfront.

★ Hostel Paradiso (300m north of the triángulo, tel. 505/2522-2878 or 8187-4542, hostelparadiso.com, paradisolaguna@hotmail.com, $10 dorm, $25-55 private, $7 for the day) is geared toward budget travelers, though you couldn't tell from looking at its beautifully landscaped property. Paradiso offers terraced patios, a floating dock, a delicious menu ($4-10), and the only bar open until 10pm in the area. Cheap transport from Granada is provided and leaves Hostel Oasis in Granada at 10am and 3pm, returning at 10:30am and 3:30pm. The dormitory has a fabulous sunrise view. This hostel organizes lots of activities during the week and offers Wi-Fi, free coffee, a volleyball court, petanque, Ping-Pong, yoga classes, windsurfing, and local crafts for sale. Ask about volunteer opportunities, or stay for a week and take Spanish classes.

The Monkey Hut (100m north of the triángulo, tel. 505/2220-3030, www.themonkeyhut.net, monkeyhulaguna@gmail.com, $14 dorm, $35-55 private room and cabaña, $6 for the day) and Laguna Beach Club (across from the triángulo, tel. 505/2520-2840, www.thelagunabeachclub.com, rememberlaguna@gmail.com, $12 dorm, $29-49 private room with fan, $6 for the day) are both found right at the entrance of the Laguna and are well-liked retreats with beautiful waterfront properties. Their recently renovated rooms provide a quiet, peaceful option for travelers. Both are popular spots for weekend day trips.

Proyecto Cocomango (500 meters north of the triángulo, tel. 550/7808-4384, proyecto-cocomango.com, CocoMango.ni@gmail.com, $90/week) is a newly formed NGO working to promote educational and artistic opportunities as well as environmental protection for the Laguna de Apoyo and nearby communities. They are always happy to have volunteers stay at their volunteer house, where you can participate in a wide variety of small projects within the community. They work closely with Hostel Paradiso, so you can also volunteer while staying at Paradiso.

The ★ Peace Project (across from the public beach entrance, tel. 505/8266-8404, U.S. 301/880-7231, $8 dorm, $14-45 private room) is an NGO that has existed in various forms since the late 1980s and under its current leadership since 2011. The organization works in the local public schools teaching English classes, as well as hosting an after-school enrichment program, which focuses on computer skills, arts, and environmental stewardship. The Peace Project hostel is on the same property as the after-school program and the proceeds of the hostel and restaurant ($3-6) go towards supporting the project. Many visitors come to the Peace Project as volunteers and spend a minimum of three weeks at the hostel or living with families, while participating in the Peace Project's programming. Since many of the folks staying at the hostel are there long-term, staying at this hostel feels like hanging out on your friend's porch. Though its property isn't lakefront, there is quick and easy access to the public beach right across the street and they'll lug a kayak to the water for you. They offer scuba lessons and Spanish classes as well. To get here, follow the well-placed signs for "Proyecto de Paz" and turn right at the school (400 meters north of the triángulo). At the end of the road, turn left and go about 100 meters.

Casa Aromansse (1.5 kilometers north of the triángulo, tel. 505/2520-2837, casaromansse.com, sergecasaromansse@gmail.com, $50-65, includes breakfast), a new bed-and-breakfast located just a bit past the public beach, is a tranquil option for travelers interested in yoga and mindfulness. Casa Aromansse has six minimalist rooms and a French-Nicaraguan restaurant that focuses on vegetarian cuisine. The owner, Serge, is a yoga instructor and massage therapist offering Thai massage and yoga and meditation classes. He also does yoga teacher training courses and yoga retreats, which are advertised on their website. Casa Aromansse has a Spanish school for guests staying a minimum of one week.

Neither hostel nor hotel, Guest House La Orquidea (1.8 kilometers north of the *triángulo,* tel. 505/8872-1866, www.laorquideanicaragua.com, $120/night for 4 people, space for up to 6 people, $10 more pp, includes breakfast, separate room $70) is a stylish two-bedroom house, fully equipped for a relaxing stay. Features include a gorgeous balcony, boats, and water toys.

On the south end of the main road, San Simian Eco-Resort (3 kilometers south of the *triángulo,* tel. 505/8850-8108, www.sansimian.com, contact@sansimian.com, $47-60, includes breakfast) is a lovely waterside group of five private bungalows, each of which has a slightly different theme, built from natural materials like thatch and bamboo. The tasteful, rustic rooms have bamboo beds with comfy mattresses, mosquito nets, fans, and fun outdoor showers and gardens. Additional features include great on-site meals, a bar, and relaxing dock with water toys. Trailheads nearby lead uphill into the jungle and along the shore.

After several years of on-and-off neglect, a new management team has taken over Apoyo Resort (1 kilometer south of the *triángulo,* tel. 505/2220-2085, U.S. 562/631-7209, www.apoyoresort.com, $70-230, includes breakfast) and is bringing the property's 60 Caribbean-style villas back to their former glory. Apartments and suites (1-3 bedrooms) have hot water, bathtubs, air-conditioning, TV/DVD, and kitchenettes. An open-air shuttle will transport you from your cabaña to one of the three restaurants, two pools, or to the lakefront (meals $7-14, Wi-Fi available). Relax by the lakeshore and swimming pools, book a massage, or go boating, biking, and hiking.

Day-trippers are welcome with a $10 minimum purchase at the restaurant.

Getting There

The Laguna de Apoyo is a 20-minute ride from either Masaya or Granada, and an hour from the airport in Managua. There are two paved roads that go up and over the crater lip and down to the water's edge: one originates on Carretera Masaya, at a spot called *el puentecito* (the 37.5 Km mark on Carretera Masaya); the other branches off the Masaya-Catarina road. They join just before passing through the village of Valle de Laguna, where you'll turn right at the T, then make a quick left to begin your descent (pay $1 if driving, unless the guardhouse is empty). The road winds downward until it forks at a pulpería. This spot is known locally as *el triángulo* (the triangle). Turn left to go north, and right to go south.

A shuttle goes from the Oasis Hostel in Granada to Hostel Paradiso in the Laguna. It leaves Granada at 10am and 3pm and returns to Granada 40 minutes later ($3 each way). You can share a taxi from Granada or Masaya for about $15. Public buses headed for the Laguna cost under $1 and leave the main Masaya market terminal at 10:30am and 3:30pm; or you can hop one of the hourly buses for Valle de Laguna, then walk (30 minutes downhill), thumb a ride, or wait for a stray taxi. There is also a cooperative of taxis that leave from the Masaya market (once they fill up) and bring you to the top of the Valle for about $0.50. These taxis are tucked away in a hidden corner of the market. If you have enough Spanish to ask around and a little time to get lost, this is the cheapest option. If you are coming from Granada or Managua on a public bus, ask to be dropped at the entrance to the Laguna (the stop is called *el puentecito*), and then catch a taxi ($4 to the bottom) or hitch a ride. Three public buses can get you back up the hill, leaving at 6:30am, 11:30am, and 4:30pm (3pm on Sun. is the last bus).

The Pueblos Blancos and Carazo

Escaping the heat of Managua or Granada is as easy as a 40-minute bus ride to the Pueblos Blancos and Carazo, two regions that occupy a breezy 500-meter-high *meseta* (plateau) south of Managua and are thus far cooler and more relaxing. The Pueblos Blancos, or White Villages, are named for the pure color of their churches (some of which, naturally, are now other colors). They are separated to the north by the Sierras de Managua, to the east by the slopes of Volcán Masaya, to the south by the Laguna de Apoyo and Volcán Mombacho, and to the west by the dry decline toward the Pacific Ocean. Each town is well known for something particular—bamboo craftwork, wicker chairs, black magic, folk dances, Sandino's birthplace, crater lakes, beaches, or interesting festivals. Visiting the pueblos is an easy day trip best appreciated if you have a car, which permits you to tour furniture workshops, coffee plantations, and outdoor plant nurseries.

In nearby Carazo, the January celebration of San Sebastián is a dramatic and colorful festival not to be missed. Jinotepe and Diriamba are laid-back towns with refreshingly cool temperatures. Carazo is also the gateway to several Pacific beaches, which are quieter than their more developed neighbors and have beautiful natural pools.

ORIENTATION

Renting a car or taxi is the best way to visit the Pueblos, but you can get around almost as easily with the *expreso* microbus system. No more than 10 or 12 kilometers separate any two towns, all of which are easily accessible from Masaya, Granada, and Managua. Buses to Nandaime, Diriá, and Diromo leave from Huembes, continue south on the Carretera Masaya, and then turn west into the hills at various points, depending on the route. The Carazo buses—to Jinotepe and Diriamba—travel via Carretera Sur and leave from the

Mercado Israel Lewites and from the UCA terminal. Also leaving from the UCA are buses that go to Diriamba heading out Carretera Masaya and turning west before Masaya. In the market in Diriamba you can catch buses to the Carazo beaches.

★ CATARINA MIRADOR

This hillside pueblo clings to the verdant lip of the spectacular Laguna de Apoyo crater lake. Catarina Mirador is a blustery cliff-side walkway and restaurant complex at the edge of the crater with one of the best panoramic views in Nicaragua. Look for the distant red-tiled roofs and cathedral spires of Granada, broad Lake Cocibolca behind, and on a clear day, the twin volcanic peaks of Ometepe. Roaming marimba and guitar players will serenade you for a small fee (negotiate before they begin playing). Locals visit Catarina for its ornamental plant nurseries and the wares of local artisans and basket makers whose shops begin at roadside. Vehicles pay $1 each to enter the *mirador* (lookout point).

Plant lovers should make sure to check out Ecovivero La Gallina (close to the entrance to the town of Catarina, tel. 505/8872-7181, tours $5 pp), an 8 manzanas (around 13 acres) plant nursery. On the property of La Gallina grow a multitude of tropical plants including rare orchids and a one-of-a-kind pink cacao plant. A family of monkeys also visits the shady property almost daily. You can arrange a tour of the property and, if you call ahead, arrangements can be made for an English-speaking guide. Don't forget bug spray! Hotel Casa Catarina (across from the central park, tel. 505/2558-0261 or 505/2558-0199, reservaciones@hotelcasacatarina.com, $45-90) is a three-star hotel with four floors and an on-site bar and restaurant. It has received mixed reviews from customers. ★ Hotel Cabañas (150m west of the Rotonda Catarina, tel. 505/2558-0484, $35) is outside of Catarina, along the highway. It has simple, charming cabañas and a swimming pool. The cabañas have air-conditioning, Wi-Fi, and cable TV; food is available if you request it in advance.

There are many restaurants within the grounds of the Catarina Mirador, which are all a little pricey and not very remarkable. Along the highway just before arriving in Catarina from Carretera Masaya is the famous restaurant **Mi Viejo Ranchito** (Km 39.5 Carretera Masaya-Catarina, tel. 505/2558-0473, miviejoranchito.com, $4-12), which has another location closer to Managua on Carretera Masaya itself. This restaurant serves high-quality traditional Nicaraguan food under a palm frond roof. It is known for its *quesillos,* a corn tortilla with fresh *quesillo* cheese (similar to string cheese), cream, and onions in vinegar on top. The Caballo Bayo sampler plate is a great way to try a variety of Nicaraguan specialties at once.

★ SAN JUAN DE ORIENTE

The community of San Juan de Oriente has been famous for its pottery for as long as anyone can remember. Nearby communities once poked fun at people from San Juan, calling

them "comebarros" ("clay eaters") for their tendency to eat off of homemade clay plates. Recent generations of San Juan potters have expanded their craft and now make attractive ceramic vases, pots, plates, and more, in both a proud celebration of pre-Columbian styles and modern inspirations. Shop at one of the small cooperatives along the entrance to town, like **Quetzalcoatl Cooperative** (coopquetzalcoatl.jimdo.com), which also offers tours and lodging, or in the many tiny displays in people's homes as you walk through the narrow streets. Many artisans are glad to invite you back into their workshops for a tour where you watch them throw pots on a foot-spun pottery wheel. Most potters use artisanal tools made from household items like a shoe-heel or bike spoke. Their pottery is exquisite and in these shops they sell for extremely low prices.

DIRIÁ AND DIRIOMO

Named for the indigenous Dirian people and their leader, Diriangén (the famed rebel cacique and martyr whose spilled blood at the hands of the conquistadors is immortalized in Carlos Mejía Godoy's anthem, "Nicaragua, Nicaragüita"), **Diriá** and **Diriomo** face each other on both sides of the highway. Both towns are well loved for their unique celebrations

the view from Catarina Mirador

learning to make pottery in San Juan de Oriente

throughout the year, mixing elements of pre-Columbian, Catholic, and surprising regional traditions (like the "dicking" festival in which participants smack each other with dried-out bull penises, sometimes practiced in San Juan de Oriente as well). Diriá, on the east, has a *mirador* smaller and less frequented than the more famous one at Catarina, as well as additional trails down to the Laguna de Apoyo. Across the highway, Diriomo is renowned for its sorcery: The intrepid traveler looking for a love potion or revenge should seek out one of the pueblo's *brujos* (sorcerers) or at least read the book *Sofía de los Presagios*. Diriomo has a crater overlook of its own: **Diriomito Mirador,** which occasionally offers paragliding, or *parapente* (tel. 505/2522-2009).

NIQUINOHOMO

Niquinohomo, "the valley of the warriors" in Nahuatl, produced a famous warrior indeed: Augusto César Sandino, born there at the turn of the 20th century. Sandino's childhood home off the northwest corner of the park has been restored as a library and museum. A 4,000-pound, solid bronze statue of the man, with the famous hat and bandolier of bullets around his waist, stands at attention at the east side of town. Niquinohomo's 320-year-old church is also worth a look.

MASATEPE

Masatepe (Nahuatl for "place of the deer") is a quiet pueblo of 12,000 that explodes in revelry the first Sunday in June during its famous **Hípica** (horse parade). Stick around after the festivities for a steaming bowl of Masatepe's culinary claim to fame: *sopa de mondongo* (cow tripe soup, washed with lime and cooked slowly in broth with vegetables), served hot in front of the town's gorgeous, architecturally unique church. Their *fiestas patronales* honor La Santísima Trinidad, the black Christ icon a Chorotegan found in the trunk of a tree during the years of the Spanish colony.

Outside of the city, both sides of the highway are lined with the workshops of the extraordinarily talented Masatepe carpenters, whose gorgeous handcrafted hardwood and rattan furniture is prized throughout the country. You'll wish you could fit more of it in your luggage (a set of chairs and a coffee table go for about $100), but console yourself instead with a comfortable, old-fashioned hardwood rocking chair. They'll disassemble and pack it down to airline-acceptable size for you for a small fee.

If driving to Masatepe from the south, save time for a meal at **Mi Teruño Masatepino** (on the east side of the road, just north of the turnoff for Pio XII and Nandasmo, tel. 505/8887-4949, $4-10), a delicious open-air restaurant featuring Nicaragua's traditional country cuisine.

MARIPOSA ECO-HOTEL AND SPANISH SCHOOL

Tucked into the forest off the road to the village of San Juan de la Concepción (a.k.a. La Concha, 12 kilometers west of Ticuantepe, under an hour from Managua), this unique hideaway has spurred a stream of rave reviews. **Mariposa Eco-Hotel and Spanish School** (tel. 505/8669-9455, www.mariposa-panishschool.com, average cost $350-400 pp per week all-inclusive) uses all of its revenue to fund a range of grassroots environmental and community projects. Guests are invited to help with the projects, from reforestation and chicken raising, to literacy, education, and animal rescue. The hotel and rooms, which use solar power, have excellent views of Volcán Masaya. There is an organic farm with coffee, bananas, free-range eggs, and lots of fruit. Meals are mostly vegetarian. Food that is not grown on their farm is bought as locally as possible. The rooms are decorated with local handicrafts, each with their own bathroom and fan. There is a fully stocked library, quality one-on-one Spanish school, and lots and lots of dogs. The school doubles as a dog shelter, so there is a constant stream of animals running around. There are volunteer and homestay opportunities as well. The all-inclusive Spanish school packages vary based on your interests.

CARAZO

Carazo is a group of small cities with refreshing cool temperatures that favor coffee production. The towns of Diriamba and Jinotepe make delightful lunch stopovers. From Diriamba you can reach the Carazo beaches, whose coastline is lined with huge rock formations and natural pools.

Jinotepe and Diriamba
DIRIAMBA

Diriamba's **Festival of San Sebastián** (third week of Jan.) is a religious, theatrical, folklore celebration uninterrupted since colonial days. Diriamba's celebration of the Holy Martyr San Sebastián stands above other pueblos' *fiestas patronales* as Nicaragua's most authentic connection to its indigenous roots. Featuring both pagan and Catholic elements, it is without rival in western Nicaragua, comparable perhaps only to Bluefield's Palo de Mayo. The festival's Dance of Toro Huaco is of indigenous ancestry and

features peacock feather hats and a multi-generational snake dance, with the youngest children bringing up the rear and an old man with a special tambourine and whistle up front. El Güegüense, also called the Macho Ratón, is recognizable for its masks and costumes depicting burdened-down donkeys and the faces of Spanish conquistadors. The Güegüense (from the old word güegüe, which means something like grumpy old man) is a hard-handed social satire with cleverly vulgar undertones that depicts the indigenous peoples' first impression of the Spanish—it has been called the oldest comedy act on the continent. UNESCO named the Güegüense dance a Masterpiece of the Oral and Intangible Heritage of Humanity. Be sure to try the official beverage of the festival: *chicha con genibre,* a ginger-tinted, slightly fermented cornmeal drink. Most of the masks and costumes in the productions are also for sale, as are homemade action figures depicting the various dance characters.

Visit the **Museo Ecológico de Trópico Seco** (in front of the police station, near the hospital, tel. 505/2534-2129, Mon.-Fri. 8am-noon and 2pm-4pm, $0.76 foreigners, $0.30 Nicas) for background on the region's unique dry tropical ecosystem. The MARENA office here ministers some of the local turtle-nesting refuges.

Hotel Mi Bohio (tel. 505/2534-4020, hotelmibohio.com, $35-70, includes breakfast) is a new hotel located in a colonial house near the museum with clean bright rooms, spa services, and one of the best restaurants in town on-site. **Restuarante Mi Bohio** (tel. 505/2534-2437, noon-9pm daily, $7-9) is a very typical Nicaraguan restaurant serving high-quality meat and seafood dishes.

Outside of town on the road to Managua, the ★ **Eco Lodge El Jardín Tortuga Verde** (tel. 505/2534-2948 or 505/8905-5313, www.ecolodgecarazo.com, rorappal@turbonett.com.ni, $25-45) is truly a pleasant and quirky guesthouse and plant nursery whose six clean, comfortable rooms are built around a beautiful jungle-like garden filled with statues. The

Nicaragua's First Microbrewery

Nicaragua's two basic beers, Victoria and Toña, dominate the beer industry. They are very light beers with only slightly different flavors that are refreshing served ice-cold, and well loved in Nicaragua. Inspired by the wide variety of microbrews he found in Seattle, a young Nicaraguan microbiologist started Cervecera Moropotente together with his brother-in-law in 2012. The brewery, "El Negrito," is located in Dolores, a small town near Jinotepe and Diriamba in Carazo. They have yet to set up tasting facilities on-site. At the time of publication, they were brewing a stout called "Lado Oscuro" (a creative combination of flavors including chocolate and coffee), a Blonde Ale called "19 Días," and a Pale Ale called "Citrus," in which they're experimenting with adding local fruits. And they've got a stockpile of recipes just waiting to be rotated into circulation.

Try the beer for yourself at one of two highly recommended restaurants near Jinotepe: Makimaki (from the University stoplight, 1 block east, 1 block south, half a block east), a reasonably priced sushi joint in Jinotepe; or Casa del Campo (Km 61 Carretera Nandaime), a classy restaurant that uses organic vegetables from its on-site organic garden.

You can find Moropetente's brews in Managua at Layha Bistro (in Altamira, from ProNicaragua, 1 block southeast), Pia Bistro, Basil Bistro, Terraza Peruana, and Embassy Bar (in Zona Hippos); in Granada at Garden Café and Oshea's; in San Juan del Sur at La Carreta (in front of Iguana); in León at Yavoy (50 meters west of Parque La Merced) and Vía Vía; and in Masaya at Frankfurt.

staff can show you around their converted coffee plantation, now rife with lush flowers and vegetation.

Go to the Centro Comercial Gutierrez (on the southeast corner of the San Sabastián Basilica) shopping center for a variety of food options, including La Nani Café, serving quality Nicaraguan dishes, panini, and waffles. Fratello's Italian restaurant is upstairs, as is Tsunami & Grill, which is popular on weekends.

JINOTEPE

Jinotepe (Xilotepetl, or "field of baby corn") is a sometimes-sleepy, sometimes-bustling villa of 27,000 set around La Iglesia Parroquial de Santiago (built in 1860) and a lively park shaded by the canopy of several immense hardwood trees. Thanks to a branch of UNAN, Jinotepe's student population keeps things youthful and lively, and its outdoor market is fun. Don't miss the beautiful two-block-long mural on the nursing school (3 blocks west of the park's northwest corner) and the towering statue of Pope John Paul II in front of the church. While you're there, enjoy an icy, chocolatey *cacao con leche* in the kiosk under the shade trees of one of Nicaragua's shadiest parks.

The Hotel Casa Mateo (1 block north of the park and 2 west, tel. 505/2532-3284, U.S. tel. 410/878-2252, hotelcasamateo.com, $15 dorm, $40-65 private room, includes breakfast) has 40 rooms with TV, private bath, hot water, and fan. There's also laundry service, a guard for your car, a restaurant (called Jardín de los Olivos), conference room, and Wi-Fi. This is a nonprofit hotel run by Glenn and Lynne Schweitzer, pastors and missionaries from Maryland, to help fund Quinta Esperanza, a home for abused and orphaned children, preschool, and vocational center. They offer special group rates ($15-20 pp).

There are dozens of small, decent eateries. Managua expats actually drive here to enjoy ★ Pizzería Coliseo (1 block north of Bancentro, tel. 505/2532-2150 or 505/2532-2646, Tues.-Fri. noon-2:30pm and 6pm-10pm, from $6), a legitimate Italian restaurant run by Rome *originario* Fausto, who's been preparing delicious pizzas and pasta in Jinotepe for more than 20 years. ★ Tian Lan Zu Shi (1.5 blocks south of the UNAN turret, tel. 505/8739-2681, Mon.-Sat. 10am-4pm, $2-3) is a delicious and reasonably priced lunch buffet of creative vegetarian Chinese dishes, sometimes with a Nicaraguan touch. **Restaurante Hípico** is a cowboy-themed rancho found just outside of town, which serves authentic Nicaraguan specialties like *sopa de mondongo* (cow tripe soup) on Mondays and *sopa de albondigas* (chicken dumplings with corn meal) on Fridays.

GETTING THERE AND AWAY

Sleek *interlocal* microbuses leave for both Jinotepe and Carazo from the UCA in Managua until 9pm. Much slower *rutas* leave from Terminal Israel Lewites.

From Jinotepe, buses leave from the COOTRAUS terminal (along the Pan-American Highway directly north of the park) at all hours for Managua, Masaya, Nandaime, and Rivas. Microbuses ($1) to Managua leave from the unofficial Sapasmapa terminal on the south side of the Instituto Alejandro, 4:45am-7:30pm. The most comfortable choice is one of the *interlocales* to Diriamba and San Marcos queued up on the street 20 meters north of the Super Santiago. Only the front one will load passengers, departing when the van is full.

From Diriamba, a fleet of *interlocales* run

to and from Jinotepe (about $0.25), daily 6am-9pm, from a spot right next to the clock tower. Walk east and take your first left to find *microbus expresos* ($1) to Managua's Mercado Israel Lewites and the UCA, 5am-8pm daily. A little farther east at the first *caseta* (booth) on the left, you can ask about all the buses that pass from Jinotepe (Managua: 4:30am-6pm daily; Masaya: 5am-6pm daily).

★ Carazo Beaches

La Boquita, Casares, and **Huehuete** are 35 kilometers due west of Diriamba. The road ends at the coast where you'll turn right to reach La Boquita tourist center (you'll pay a small fee to enter). A left at the coast takes you to Huehuete and Casares, which are both small fishing towns. These beaches attract mostly Nicaraguan families on picnics and outings and the odd foreigner in search of fresh fish dishes. On a big swell, the surf can be up at both places, and you'll likely be the only gringo in the lineup (rental boards are sometimes available). Just in front of MyrinaMar hotel and a very short walk south of the Boquita tourist center, the coast is lined with huge rocks that you can walk on when the tide is not at its highest. Pools form within these rocks like natural

the beach at La Boquita

whirlpool tubs with moss-carpeted flooring. Lounging in these pools is a great break from the tide and feels luxurious and peaceful. This area—particularly La Boquita—is best avoided during Semana Santa and New Year's Day when it is overrun by drunken mobs of vacationers.

When you walk into La Boquita there will be various ranchos (thatch-roofed restaurants) whose waiters will come over to try to pull you in. All of the restaurants are similar and serve good fish options. Suleyka (in the back left corner of the tourist center, $4-9) is the most relaxed of these and also has a decent hotel. Suleyka Hotel (tel. 505/8698-3355, sw-lagos@yahoo.com, $10-80) has simple rooms with air-conditioning and private bathrooms, and is right on the beach; the largest room can sleep 10 (in bunk beds). At La Boquita, there are a handful of interchangeable *hospedajes* with basic (occasionally filthy) rooms for under $15.

Just before La Boquita tourist center is an excellent B&B, MyrinaMar (del Empalme La Boquita/Casares, 1 kilometer towards la Boquita, tel. 505/8421-8306, myrinamar.com, $95-125 d). This pristine white house on the cliff in front of the beach has four beautifully designed rooms for 4-5 people. The upstairs suites have a second story loft and multi-tiered, stylish bathrooms, while the downstairs suite sleeps five in two rooms and has a fully stocked kitchen. The owners are two French doctors, one of whom is also a massage therapist who offers massage and acupuncture. They serve a superb multi-course breakfast using Nicaragua's tropical fruit varieties in creative ways.

Public transportation leaves from the main market on the highway east of the clock tower in Diriamba. Express microbuses leave every 20 minutes 6:20am-6pm daily for the ride to La Boquita (40 minutes, $0.75). Ordinario buses take 90 minutes and leave 6:40am-6:30pm daily. From the beach at La Boquita, buses depart 5am-6pm daily.

La Isla de Ometepe and San Juan del Sur

South of Managua, the land crumples into high cloudy ridges and the windblown peak of Las Nubes, and then falls off slowly until it spills into southwestern Nicaragua's plains. Here, Lake Cocibolca presses the land into a narrow belt

that barely separates the lake from the Pacific Ocean.

By the time the Spanish "discovered" this region, the Nicaraos (Uto-Aztecan people of southwestern Nicaragua) had been residents for at least seven generations. The modern day department of Rivas in southern Nicaragua is home to two of the major draws for tourists in the country—the alluring Isla de Ometepe and the beautiful Pacific coastal beaches.

These days, the town of Rivas is a transportation hub that draws less attention than the coastal communities of Tola and San Juan del Sur and La Isla de Ometepe, though it retains a colonial charm appreciated by many. But it's hard to compete with Ometepe for attention. The magnificent twin-peaked island rises like a crown from the center of Lake Cocibolca. An intensely volcanic island steeped in tradition and mystery, Ometepe was the ancestral home of the Nahuatl people and today is an alluring destination for

travelers, with its sandy beaches, swimming holes, hiking trails, and, of course, two breathtaking volcanoes: one hot, one cold (the former remains quite active).

Meanwhile on the coast, sunsets continue to paint the silhouettes of fishing vessels in crimson, and the mood in San Juan del Sur is low-key and fun. The noon sun is scorching, so life is languorous and measured, spent swinging in breezy hammocks, enjoying fresh fish and cold beer at seaside, or splashing about in the surf. While San Juan del Sur is the largest beach town, there is a host of less party-heavy alternatives up and down the coast.

PLANNING YOUR TIME

La Isla de Ometepe should not be missed on any but the shortest trips to Nicaragua. It offers in a nutshell a little of everything Nicaragua has to offer, from history to waterfalls and volcanic trekking to horseback

Highlights

© AVALON TRAVEL

★ **Río Istián:** Paddling a kayak through these still waters early in the morning or during sunset is a breathtaking experience (page 66).

★ **Volcán Maderas:** The lower slopes of this volcano are covered with petroglyphs dating from before Columbus (page 67).

★ **Cascada San Ramón:** The most popular attraction by far on Ometepe's south side is this stunning 180-meter waterfall (page 71).

★ **Surfing near San Juan del Sur:** This major surf center draws shredders and groms from all over. There are waves for all levels out here, and plenty of places that offer beginner lessons (page 86).

★ **La Flor Wildlife Refuge:** Even if you miss the spectacular nighttime turtle-nesting events, a simple walk along this protected beach and up the forested river is remarkable (page 97).

★ **Playa Marsella:** Gentle waves and a secluded beach make for all sorts of opportunities (page 99).

★ **Playa Gigante:** This magical little beach town, nestled in a beautiful, calm bay, is surrounded by some of the best beaches in the country (page 102).

★ **Charco Verde Reserve:** Verdant and cool, this gorgeous reserve is a lovely little ecosystem with a sandy lakeshore beach in the shadows of tall trees (page 60).

La Isla de Ometepe and San Juan del Sur

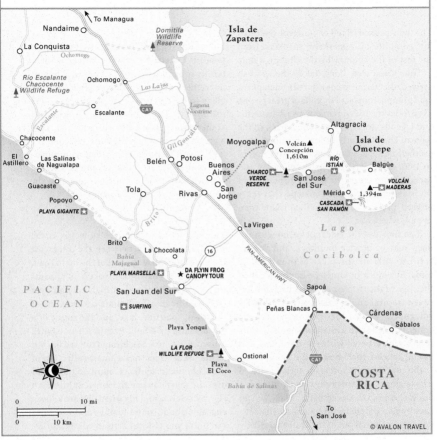

OMETEPE AND SAN JUAN DEL SUR

riding, all in an environment travelers routinely rave about as relaxing and delightful. You could feasibly travel to and from the island in a single day, but such a short trip would be folly. Rather, allow at least two days and two nights (and an extra day and night if you'd like to hike a volcano, which is a full day activity in itself). Travel in this region requires careful coordination of transport, as you can easily lose up to a half day waiting for boats and buses. Traveling around Ometepe is never easy; local transport is slow and erratic (especially on Sundays) and

renting vehicles can be expensive. If you're visiting the island in February, when the annual Survival Run occurs, book rooms well in advance.

San Juan del Sur proper is a relatively small town; you could walk every street in a single morning. Most visitors spend at least two days and a night here. Beach lovers and surfers can stretch it into a full week using the town as a base to explore the surrounding beaches and coves. Buses, taxis, and shuttles in Rivas connect with most of the beach destinations to the north and south.

La Isla de Ometepe

The twin-peaked island of Ometepe (Nahuatl for "two hills") is remarkably insulated from the rest of the country by the choppy waters of Lake Cocibolca. Long before the Spanish arrived, the islanders considered Ometepe sacred ground, inhabited by gods of great power. Even today the island remains awash in myths and legends, some of which date back to the days of the Nahuatl. Today's islanders prefer their home to what they call "over there." In 1957, as Volcán Concepción rumbled and threatened to erupt, the government ordered the islanders to evacuate Ometepe; they flatly refused, preferring to die on their island than live anywhere else.

The slopes of the volcanoes echo with the deep roar of howler monkeys, and the air is filled with the sharp cry of thousands of birds. Ecologically, Ometepe has been called the edge of the tropics, as a dividing line between tropical and dry falls between the two volcanoes. Volcán Maderas is extinct. Its crater is filled with a shallow lagoon and its slopes are carpeted with more tropical and humid species, including actual cloud forest at the top. Concepción is an active volcano whose slopes are covered with tropical dry forest species. On December 8, 1880, Volcán Concepción erupted with such force that lava and smoke flowed out of the crater for nearly a year. The most recent mini-eruption was in 2011.

Ometepe's proud residents live a mostly agrarian lifestyle on the slopes of the twin Cenozoic volcanoes. The two principal towns, Moyogalpa and Altagracia, are formerly sleepy port towns and transportation hubs enjoying an upswing in tourism. Costs are lower here than on the neighboring Pacific coast. Many isolated areas on the island do not accept credit cards; take advantage of the ATMs available in town before heading out.

MOYOGALPA

Moyogalpa (Nahuatl for "place of the mosquitoes") is Ometepe's largest commercial center. In spite of its name, it's not that buggy, but rather a growing little town that's an easy place to base your trip, especially if you're planning to climb Concepción. The town sits at the western base of the volcano, making it a great place to watch the sunset beyond the lake. You'll find plenty of fine accommodations and food here, but I recommend basing yourself outside of the town to experience the more isolated sides of the island.

Sights

The best spot to watch the sunset is at the small lakeside park between the docks. At the top of the hill at the end of the main road, Moyogalpa's Catholic church is charming, with a bell tower just high enough over the tree line to afford you a decent view of the town, coastline, lake, and the statue of a boy urinating. La Sala Arqueológica (or El Museo, 9am-5pm, $1), located toward the top of the main street, has a small collection of pre-Columbian artifacts found on the island over the years. Owner and amateur historian Herman García and his wife Ligia are knowledgeable about island history and lore, and can point you to local artisan communities. The store in front of the museum sells contemporary works. Walk one kilometer along the lakeshore north of town to arrive at the wetlands and lagoon of El Apante. In the dry season, enjoy its rich birdlife while walking the nature trail around the lagoon.

Entertainment and Events

La Esquina Caliente (on the main street) is a popular place to drink and relax—good luck getting a table on game night. You'll find the weekend dancing crowd at Disco Johnny Bar (just north of the dock).

La Isla de Ometepe

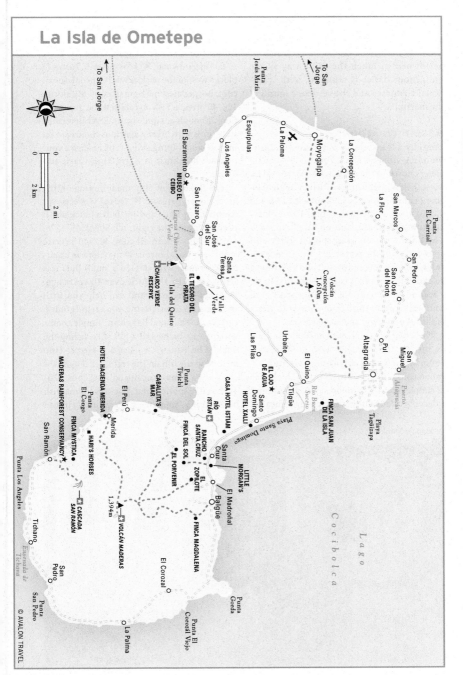

0
0
2 km
2 mi

To San Jorge

To San Jorge

Punta Jesús María

Esquipulas

La Paloma

Los Angeles

El Sacramento

MUSEO EL CEBO

San Lázaro

Moyogalpa

La Concepción

Volcán Concepción 1,610m

San Marcos

La Flor

San José del Norte

San Pedro

San José del Sur

San José del Sur

Santa Teresa

EL TESORO DEL PIRATA

Isla del Quiste

CHARCO VERDE RESERVE

Laguna Charco Verde

Valle Verde

Las Pilas

Urbaite

Punta El Carrizal

San Pedro

San Miguel

Puerto Altagracia

Altagracia

Playa Tagüitapa

El Quino

Tilgüe

Santo Domingo

HOTEL XALLI

EL OJO DE AGUA

CASA HOTEL ISTIAM

RÍO ISTIÁN

Río Buen Suceso

FINCA SAN JUAN DE LA ISLA

Playa Santo Domingo

Punta Tichiti

CABALLITA'S MAR

El Perú

HOTEL HACIENDA MÉRIDA

Punta El Congo

MADERAS RAINFOREST CONSERVANCY

Mérida

FINCA MYSTICA

HARI'S HORSES

San Ramón

CASCADA SAN RAMÓN

1,394m

VOLCÁN MADERAS

FINCA DEL SOL

RANCHO SANTA CRUZ

EL PORVENIR

EL ZOPILOTE

Santa Cruz

Balgüe

LITTLE MORGAN'S

El Madroñal

FINCA MAGDALENA

El Corozal

Lago Cocibolca

Punta Gorda

Punta El Corozal Viejo

San Pedro

La Palma

Punta San Pedro

Ensenada de Tichana

Tichana

Punta Los Angeles

© AVALON TRAVEL

The town of Moyogalpa celebrates its patron saint, Santa Ana, June 23-26, with the Baile de las Inditas. This dance is performed in much the same way as the indigenous dance it replaced, with traditional costumes and the resonant sound of the marimba.

Accommodations

Consider a homestay in Moyogalpa and surrounding villages. The Landing Hotel (100 meters north of the dock, tel. 505/2569-4113, www.thelandinghotel.com, thelandinghotel@gmail.com, $7 dorm, $5 hammock, $15 s, $20 d, $30 apartments, $40 cabin) has a pleasant common space, and an attentive staff. The dorms are nothing special (dark and cramped), but the private rooms are a good value (ask for one on the second floor for a volcano view). There's garden space out back, a second floor hammock lounge with gym equipment, and a third floor patio with views of the lake and Volcán Concepción.

Hotelito Aly (1.5 blocks north of the dock on the left, tel. 505/2569-4196 or 505/8686-0830, www.hotelitoaly.com, hotelitoaly@yahoo.com, $7 dorm, $10 pp private bath) has 11 simple rooms set around a garden patio and a decent restaurant that serves three meals a day. The rooms feel a bit unfinished, but the family is friendly and helpful. The second floor balcony has a nice view of the volcano.

German-owned ★ Hospedaje Soma (3 blocks west of the park, www.hospedajesoma.com, hospedajesoma@gmail.com, $10 dorm, $20-40 private, $50-60 cabin) is the nicest option, although not quite central. Whitewashed structures with breezy, spacious rooms are set in lush landscaping. All guests receive a continental breakfast of eggs, fruit, toast, and coffee.

You'll feel right at home lounging on the breezy open patio at ★ Hotel Ometepetl (across from The Landing, half a block north of the dock on the right, tel. 505/2569-4276, ometepetlng@hotmail.com, $12-40 private bath, a/c). Local owner Doña Nora is a self-made woman who started a small business selling food by the dock over 40 years ago. Her staff is friendly and can help you with the logistics of preparing your trip (guides, cars, etc.). The hotel has clean, simple rooms with private baths and a gift shop facing the dock. The American Café & Hotel (100 meters up the hill on the right, tel. 505/8645-7193, www.americancafeandhotel.com, $20-40) has five spotless and spacious rooms with high ceilings, hot water, and reasonably priced

Hospedaje Soma

gringo-style breakfasts (café: daily 7am-4pm). The Cornerhouse (1 block north of the dock, www.thecornerhouseometepe.com, $25 s, $35 d) has a small sunny B&B above the café with cozy rooms.

Food

All the aforementioned accommodations serve food, including homemade Nica meals, the nicest of which is found at the restaurant at Ometepetl (across from The Landing, half a block north of the dock on the right, daily 7am-8pm, $2-5). Los Ranchitos (4 blocks up the hill from the dock, then half a block south, tel. 505/2569-4112, daily 7am-9:30pm, large pizza $6) is a favorite among locals and Peace Corps volunteers; its huge menu features surprisingly good pizza.

The trendy ★ Cornerhouse (1 block north of the dock, www.cornerhouseometepe.com, Mon.-Sat. 7am-5pm, $3-6) has one of the best breakfast selections in town. Expect local coffee (from an espresso machine), fresh-baked bread, granola and jam made from scratch, and refreshing smoothies. They also sell *artesanía* (crafts) from local women's co-ops, who receive 100 percent of the sales.

Restaurante La Galería (2 blocks from the dock on the main road, daily 3:30pm-10pm, $4-10) serves delicious pasta dishes in a mellow atmosphere. Enjoy the art on the walls and smooth music while you wait on the sometimes-slow service. The bar/restaurant ★ El Indio Viejo (inside the Hospedaje Central, $3-7) offers smoothies, fish sandwiches, gringo burgers, burritos, and of course, *indio viejo* (a traditional corn-based stew). This is one of the only places I've found in the country where you can try a vegetarian version of the popular national dish. A good portion of their food is farm-to-table and organic, straight from their nearby *finca* (farm).

Information and Services

Get oriented at the Unión de Guías de Ometepe, or UGO (located to the left of the dock, tel. 505/8241-1794 or 505/8827-7714, daily 8am-5pm). This professional collective has enabled the local guides to share knowledge, formalize their training, and get sharp-looking uniforms to boot. Stop in and ask about bus schedules or places to stay. The offices for Cacique Tours (1 block up the hill, tel. 505/8417-8692) are equally knowledgeable and helpful. Both have INTUR-certified guides and can organize your volcano hike or island tour.

There are four banks in town, three of

Try vegetarian versions of popular national dishes at El Indio Viejo.

Alternative Tourism on Ometepe

There are numerous opportunities to support everyday Nicaraguans with your tourism dollars. From long-standing solidarity partnerships to sustainable agriculture work and research projects, Ometepe awaits those looking for something a little different.

HOMESTAYS AND COMMUNITY TOURISM

There are a handful of community-based tourism projects around the island. Experience authentic Nicaraguan living and invest in community tourism by spending a night with one of the families of **Puesta del Sol** (in the village of La Paloma, a few kilometers south of Moyogalpa, tel. 505/8619-0219 or 505/8695-7768, www.puestadelsol.org, $25/night). Accommodation rates include three home-cooked meals and filtered water. All bedrooms have a fan and access to toilets, but you'll share common spaces with dogs, chickens, and curious children. Rent a kayak or bike, and hang out in the small waterfront café. Learn to make *comida típica* in cooking classes ($10 pp), and try some of the locally made hibiscus wine. Basic Spanish will make your stay more enjoyable as the families involved don't speak much English. (Someone in the community does speak French, however.)

Pueblo Hotel Los Angeles (tel. 505/2569-4611 or 505/5720-1542, contact Carolina Flores Morales, pueblometepe1@gmail.com, $20/night pp) is a network of 15 women in the community of Los Angeles who host tourists in their homes. The cost of a stay includes three meals per day and a complete immersion experience. Aside from traditional tourism activities offered elsewhere on the island, the Pueblo Hotel members can arrange tours and a local youth organization rents bicycles.

At the foot of Volcán Maderas, **Mujeres de Balgüe** (tel. 505/8656-0857 or 505/8897-5035, trc. mujeresbalgue@yahoo.com, $8 pp) is a group of women who open their homes to guests. You'll get your own private room and you can arrange meals ($3 breakfast, $4 lunch, $4.50 dinner) with your family. It's best to arrange in advance, but once in Balgüe, you can check for availability at Comedor Isabel.

In Moyogalpa, **Escuela Hotel Teosintal** (2 blocks east of the dock, teosintalometepe09@ yahoo.es, $20 d) aims to provide an additional source of income for local producers and improve customer service and tourism services on the island. The theory is reinforced by the students' interaction with hotel guests. The hotel can arrange tours around the island or up to the volcanoes. The project, operating since 2005, can connect you with a network of agricultural cooperatives, many of which specialize in the production of sesame seeds for export.

which are located on the main strip (BAC, Banpro, and Bancentro). The **hospital** (3 blocks east of the park along the highway out of town, tel. 505/2569-4247) is more of a health center. For more serious ailments and injuries, go to the hospital in Rivas.

NEAR MOYOGALPA

La Concepción

More commonly referred to as "La Concha," this community three kilometers north of Moyogalpa is the start of one of the active volcano's more accessible trails. **Finca María Andrea** (tel. 505/8659-8964, $2 camping, plus $5 to rent a tent) is a working family farm accustomed to serving breakfast to early morning hikers.

San Marcos

Just northeast of Moyogalpa along the "back way around the island" is the small community of San Marcos, home to a women's group that makes and sells ceramic pieces, including authentic replicas of pre-Columbian art. Ask around in town for the *taller de artesanía*.

Punta Jesús María

The long, sandy peninsula of Punta Jesús

VOLUNTEER OPPORTUNITIES

In the community of Santa Cruz, you'll find the Fundación Entre Volcánes (tel. 505/2569-4118, www.fundacionentrevolcanes.org, lorenaazteca41@yahoo.es), which runs projects all over Volcán Maderas focusing on environmental education, agriculture, and sustainable tourism. Opportunities range from assisting with school workshops to farm work and teaching composting techniques. You could also assist with community tourism trainings and marketing. Your Spanish should be at least conversational. Time commitments depend on the project.

In 2007, the folks at Hacienda Mérida founded the Ometepe Bilingual School (on the southwestern side of the island, tel. 505/8868-8973, contact Alvaro Molina, www.hmerida.com, alvaronica@gmail.com), a free afterschool English-language program for children in the rural community of Mérida. The school hosts international volunteers; student groups and individuals come from around the world. You can teach English to local elementary and high school students. There is a two-week minimum commitment, a $125 fee, and accommodations with a local family, or in the dormitories at Hacienda Mérida.

The Maderas Rainforest Conservancy (formerly the Ometepe Biological Field Station, Miami tel. 305/666-9932, www.maderasrfc.org, info@maderasrfc.org) is located near Merida, on the slopes of Volcán Maderas. They manage numerous forward-thinking conservation projects in surrounding communities, including a botanical garden on the lakeshore to serve as a refuge for endangered Blue Morpho butterflies. They also operate a field school for birding groups and research students. Tourists are welcome to sample the restaurant or stay at the station for a small fee.

AGRI-TOURISM

To learn about organic agriculture, permaculture, and horticulture, spend a couple of weeks at Finca Bona Fide (about 300 meters left of Finca Magdalena, tel. 505/8616-4566, www.projectbonafide.com, $20/night, less if you stay more than 1 week). Chris runs a beautiful farm, offers 18-day organic agriculture workshops (free for locals), has a nutritional kitchen in Balgüe, and offers farm work internships. Enjoy rustic lodging (a bunk bed or hammock on a raised platform) and three meals a day. Advance arrangements are preferred.

Similar agricultural work arrangements can be made at La Finca Ecológica El Zopilote (tel. 505/2560-1764, www.ometepezopilote.com). If you'll be sticking around more than a couple of weeks, ask about discounts. Finally, check out the Fincas Verdes network (www.fincasverdes.com) to get a lowdown on the various agricultural and conservation ventures being offered on the island.

María is lovely for swimming and relaxing in the dry season and submerges in the rainy season. The narrow kilometer-long sandbar is a good place to watch the sun set or enjoy a meal after a swim in the lake. The entrance is a long driveway just north of the town of Esquipulas that takes 15 minutes to walk. Take the bus and ask to get off at the picturesquely named Punta de la Paloma (Dove's Point). Don't leave bikes or valuables unattended here, as robberies aren't unheard of.

Stay nearby at ★ Finca Samaria (2 kilometers south of Punta la Paloma, tel. 505/8824-2210 or 505/8636-4886, $4 camp, $3

hammock, beachfront cabin $15, rooms $15-25) in Los Angeles. Rooms aren't fancy, but they're clean. Owners can organize fishing, horseback riding, and volcano tours. If you're just on a day trip, it's worth stopping for farm-to-table goodness at their restaurant Playa Samaritano (6am-9pm daily, $2-11), where you'll find homemade bread, paneer cheese and tofu, and delicious vegan options in addition to hamburgers and steak chimichurri.

Museo El Ceibo

Eight kilometers outside Moyogalpa in El Sacramento are the archaeological and currency museums at Museo El Ceibo (tel. 505/8874-8076, elceibomuseos.com, daily 8am-5pm, $5 each, $8 for both). The ranch was once a tobacco farm, and the archaeological museum is housed in the cellar formerly used for drying tobacco. The collection includes over 1,500 well-preserved pre-Columbian pieces from across the island, including unearthed funerary urns, jewelry, weapons, and tools of the Nahuatl dating back to AD 3000. The currency museum includes samples of Nicaraguan money dating all the way back to cacao—the only coin you can eat. Make a day of it: grab a bite at the Bar La Herradura (daily 7am-9pm, $3-8) followed by a languid dip in the lake. Or stay in one of the appealing new cabins ($68 d with a/c) and unwind in the large, well-maintained pool and enjoy free museum admission.

★ Charco Verde Reserve

Swim in the lake accompanied only by the call of the monkeys in the treetops and the whir of colorful birds. This is still a relatively wild area, with enough tall trees remaining to harbor some exciting wildlife. The entire area has been cordoned off to prevent development, leaving this cove an oasis of peace. Pay $2 to walk along one of three trails (totaling 4km) in the private nature reserve, one each for beginner, intermediate, and advanced experience levels. The easiest hike is flat and wheelchair accessible. You'll have amazing panoramic views of the island, and may see (or at least hear) howler monkeys, birds, and other wildlife. Bring bug spray. There is a lagoon in the reserve, but it's not recommended for swimming as it's full of algae.

According to legend, the enchanted city of Chico Largo lies beneath the lagoon. Some say that Chico Largo appears to people at night and offers to make a deal: wealth and prosperity during life, in exchange for their souls, which upon death, he converts into cattle. Many of the cows on the island, then, are the souls of Ometepe's previous generation, which opted for a life of decadence

pre-Columbian pieces at Museo El Ceibo

instead of hard work. In another version of the legend, the cacique Nicarao is buried with his solid gold throne along the edge of the Charco Verde. In this version, Chico Largo is a descendant of Nicarao and roams the area guarding and protecting Nicarao's tomb, as well as Ometepe's wildlife.

Some 50 meters from the reserve entrance is the Paraíso de las Mariposas (daily 7am-5pm, $5) butterfly reserve. Enjoy the beautifully landscaped garden before moving into the screened-in refuge, which houses 14 species of butterflies, including the endangered Blue Morpho. The entrance fee includes a peek at the on-site laboratory and an explanation of caterpillar transformation.

On Cerro Mogote, 100 meters down the road from the Charco Verde entrance, is La Mirador del Diablo. This hill is the highest point between the two volcanoes and provides excellent views. Hike up the short trail ($1 to access) to the lookout point, or do a canopy tour (tel. 505/8656-0522, daily 8:30am-4:30pm, $25 pp), which consists of 15 stations, a Tarzan swing, hanging bridge, and a 20-meter-high free fall or rappel.

ACCOMMODATIONS

The three nearest hotels are each owned by a different Riveras sibling. Each rents horses and offers boat and kayak trips along the shoreline, fishing trips, and horseback riding. Hotel y Restaurante Charco Verde (next to the reserve entrance, tel. 505/8887-9302 or 505/2560-1271, www.charcoverde.com.ni, charcoverde22@yahoo.es, $35-92) has easy trail access. Cute cabanas with tile floors, sunny windows, front porch, private bath, and air-conditioning can fit up to six people. The big lakefront restaurant has an air of luxury.

Up the beach is Hotel Finca Venecia (tel. 505/8887-0191 or 505/2560-1269, fincavenecia.com, hotelfincavenecia@yahoo.com, $25-50 cabin), a family-style guesthouse on a hundred-year-old farm on the beach. All rooms have hot water and air-conditioning. Ask for a lakefront cabin and watch the sunset from your private terrace. The restaurant serves well-prepared pasta, chicken, fish, and beef dishes. From here, it's an easy walk along the shore into the reserve of Charco Verde and to Playa Balcón. Right next door is La Posada de Chico Largo (tel. 505/8886-4069 or 505/8473-7210, chicolargo@yahoo.com, $10 dorm beds, $30 d), the most economic of the three. Despite their nickname, "Los Diablos" are accommodating hosts and their restaurant is good.

Valle Verde

The pirate's treasure is, in this case, an isolated retreat on a wide, black-sand beach rather off the beaten track. Reach the cove by getting off the bus at the entrance just beyond San José del Sur, then walking 15 minutes from the highway, following the signs. El Tesoro del Pirata (tel. 505/8927-2831 or 505/8566-8782, tesorodelpirata@gmail.com, $25 cabana, $5 pp camping) is located just far enough off the beaten track to encourage the local wildlife to whoop it up for you. Cabins are simple with private baths and can fit up

to four people. The owners recently added a small lakefront pool for guest use. The view is excellent, as is the swimming and boating, and they serve some of the best tasting fish on the island.

ALTAGRACIA

The second largest community on Ometepe and an important island port, Altagracia is more picturesque than Moyogalpa but plays second fiddle with regard to attractions and services. In 2000, National Geographic filmed a documentary about vampire bats here. While there are indeed many vampire bats, they are a threat only to the local chickens, which the bats suck dry by hanging from the chickens' nerveless feet.

Sights

El Museo Ometepe (next to the *alcaldía,* daily 9am-5pm, $1) has a few exhibits on the flora, fauna, and archaeology of Ometepe, including statues and ceramic pieces unearthed around the island. The church courtyard across from the park makes for a peaceful retreat with a few interesting pre-Columbian stone idols for added irony. You might get yelled at by a group of bright green parakeets that make their home in the roof of the dilapidated old church (right next to the new church). Across the street in the central park, you'll find the artesanía cooperative (daily 8am-4pm), comprised of local artisans who take turns working in the kiosk. Some of the pieces are original and exhibit the pride that the islanders have for their home.

From the park, walk east down a sandy road for 30 minutes, or bike, to the bay of Playa Tagüizapa, a fine sandy beach for swimming. You can pick up supplies in town for a picnic and make a lazy day of it. Located three kilometers north of the town of Altagracia, the port has boat service between Granada and San Carlos (Río San Juan). The road that leads to the port is shady and makes a nice, short walk—allow 45 minutes each way. On the way, you'll pass Playa Paso

Hiking Ometepe's Volcanoes

Ometepe's twin peaks are a siren's call for many intrepid backpackers, and hiking one or both is an intimate way to get to know the island. But do not underestimate the difficulty of the challenge before you: Both peaks are equally dangerous, for different reasons.

On either peak, a guide is *required*, and for good reason: The "trails" are unmarked, and branch dozens of times. On Maderas, an experienced hiker got lost in the crevices of the volcano's middle slopes and succumbed to dehydration and died. I recommend using a trained local guide from UGO (tel. 505/8827-7714, ugometepe@yahoo.com). You can hire a guide starting at $40 per group. Cacique Tours (tel. 505/8417-8692, office in Moyogalpa, informational kiosk in San Jorge port) is an excellent option, providing safe, experienced guides. Berman Gómez (tel. 505/8816-6971, ometepeisland@gmail.com) was the first bilingual guide on the island, and has since worked with BBC and *Survivor*. His prices remain reasonable, and his passion for wildlife makes his tours noteworthy.

VOLCÁN CONCEPCIÓN

Volcán Concepción (1,610 m.) is the more arduous climb. Large parts of the hike are treeless, rocky scrambles. Don't be surprised if the volcano is off-limits the day you arrive, as Concepción is quite active, and has spewn gas and ash on several occasions, including as recently as March 2010. The authorities prohibit climbs when the seismologists show conditions aren't safe. As you reach the volcanic cone, the wind that buffets you is cold until you reach the crater lip, where the volcano's hot, sulphurous gas pours forth (the clash of hot and cold air is responsible for the almost permanent cloud cover at the top of the volcano). On the off chance that the clouds thin, the view from the peak is unforgettable.

Allow a whole day for the full hike: five exhausting hours up and four knee-shattering hours down. Eat a hearty breakfast; take plenty of water, food, sun protection, and good shoes and socks to protect your feet.

Most travelers hike Concepción by way of the town La Concha (La Concepción). Following this trail until the forest ends is the most accessible hike, taking about five hours up and back. After that point, the trail continues steeply up, and is not recommended for inexperienced hikers. The trails that start at La Flor and Moyogalpa both meet up with La Concha's trail. There is an eastern approach from Altagracia that leads through an impressive amount of monkey-inhabited forest before hitting the exposed section. There are two southern trails in San José del Sur and Los Ramos, which are more difficult than the others due to their steep incline.

VOLCÁN MADERAS

Volcán Maderas (1,394 m.) is more accessible, and the volcano is dormant, if not extinct (in fact, there's a forested lake within the crater). It is thus more frequently hiked, but remains

---

Real, an out-of-the-way bathing beach you'll likely have all to yourself. If you're heading to the port to catch the boat to Granada or San Carlos, it's worthwhile to speak with the owner of Hotel Central. They offer pickup truck service to the port, so you don't have to carry your luggage that far. When the water is too rough, the boat may not show up at Altagracia at all, preferring to hug the eastern shore of the lake.

Entertainment and Events

Altagracia's *fiestas patronales,* in celebration of San Diego, are held November 12-18. In addition to the traditional festivities, the Baile de las Ramas (Dance of the Branches) is a major component of the celebration. The dancers tear off smaller branches of the guanacaste tree and hold them to their heads while dancing to imitate the worker *zompopo* (leaf-cutter) ants carrying leaves off to the anthills.

Volcán Concepción is still active.

equally dangerous and is responsible for at least two deaths since 2005. Maderas is a national park above 400 meters, and for good reason: It's really beautiful up there. You'll pass petroglyphs on your way up. When you reach the crater lip, the final descent to the mist-swept crater lake requires a rope and should not be attempted without proper safety equipment—make sure your guide packs rope.

The most commonly used trail to the top starts at Finca Magdalena; if you're not staying at the Finca Magdalena you must pay a trail fee to enter and pass through the coffee plantations. You'll pass a petroglyph or two on the way up. There are also nearby trails starting at La Finca Ecológica El Zopilote and Albergue Ecológico El Porvenir. Allow 4 hours to go up and 2-3 to come back down, and count on resting an hour at the crater lake (58 minutes of which you'll spend deciding whether or not to jump in the cold, mushy-bottom *laguna*). Some guides prefer hikers not swim here due to unseen submerged tree branches, which can cause injuries.

Another, more strenuous ascent leaves from Mérida. The first three hours include petroglyphs and a spectacular view from the *mirador* (lookout) but are an almost vertical ascent, leveling off into the upper reaches that one hiker calls "enchanted." All trails meet at the same spot before descending into the crater. For folks who aren't interested in the exhausting full trek, hike halfway up the Finca Magdalena trail to a coffee and rice-producing village, Las Cajillas. Nearby is a small waterfall, Cascada El Jerusalem—less impressive than San Ramón, but still worth the hike.

Accommodations and Food

Altagracia's accommodations are generally located within a few blocks of each other, so feel free to walk around and compare before settling in. One of the cheapest and friendliest choices is Hospedaje Ortiz (a block or so from the central park, $4-5 pp). Hostal Edelma (2 blocks north of the park, tel. 505/8417-8692, $8 pp) is a bit nicer. ★ Hotel Central (2 blocks south of the park, tel. 505/2569-4420 or 505/8661-3858, doscar-flores@yahoo.es, $6 pp shared bath, $10-12 pp private) is a traveler favorite, with a nicely furnished reading room, small garden, and helpful staff.

At Hotel Castillo (tel. 505/8856-8003 or 505/2569-4403, hotelcastillo@hotmail.com, $5 pp shared bath, $10-15 private bath), the upstairs dorm has a street-side balcony.

64

Information and Services

The small **Centro de Salud** (300 meters north of the park, tel. 505/2552-6089) can treat patients 24 hours a day, but for serious injuries have the owner of your hotel take you in a vehicle to the hospital in Moyogalpa, or head for the hospital in Rivas.

NEAR ALTAGRACIA
El Quino

Stay with a local family at **Hospedaje La Peñita** (tel. 505/8972-6299, famrampaiza@yahoo.es, $4 pp). The friendly owner has bikes to rent and will take you on a guided tour of the island. To get there, take the bus from Altagracia to El Quino (at the fork for the isthmus) and walk 300 meters north. This is about as close as you can stay to El Ojo de Agua.

Finca San Juan de la Isla

The beautiful and isolated ★ **Finca San Juan de la Isla** (tel. 505/8560-6977 or 505/8886-0734, www.sanjuandelaisla.com, $75-125) provides some of the nicest lakefront lodging on the island. Prices are higher than most other places on the island. Spend your time horseback riding on the beach, kayaking in the lake, or rent a bike or scooter to visit the nearby El Ojo de Agua. A taxi from Moyogalpa runs about $20.

El Ojo de Agua

Located near the town of Tilgüe, on the northern part of the isthmus, **El Ojo de Agua** ($2) consists of crystal-clear, spring-fed waters captured in two natural, stone pools set in the middle of a gorgeous and colorful botanical garden. Swim in the revitalizing waters the way the Nahautls probably did, then climb out to drip-dry in the sun. It's the best swimming hole on the island other than the lake itself, and the water is the cleanest you'll find anywhere. Your entrance fee helps with maintenance, as does whatever you pay to take home some organic, herbal tea. Snacks (nothing fancy) are available at the little bar/shop (daily 7am-6pm). You can string up a hammock or set up a tent for the night ($3).

PLAYA SANTO DOMINGO

Playa Santo Domingo runs along the eastern side of the narrow wedge of land that connects the volcanoes of Concepción and Maderas, the product of rich volcanic soil that washed down from the slopes of both volcanoes over millennia, gradually

Playa Santo Domingo

OMETEPE AND SAN JUAN DEL SUR
LA ISLA DE OMETEPE

connecting the two islands. The several-kilometer-long stretch of black sand on the northern part of the Istián Isthmus runs alongside the pueblos of Santo Domingo, San Fernando, and Santa Cruz. Its central location makes it the most convenient base for exploring the rest of the island. The swimming can be nice, but with the near-constant onshore breeze, the water is usually choppy and it can get very windy. If there are loads of *chayules* (gnats) when you visit, consider staying on another part of the island, away from the water, where these harmless but annoying little bugs are nearly nonexistent. Also note that in the rainy season water levels rise and the sandy beach all but disappears. Any time of year, expect great views of both volcanoes.

Athletes should check out the **Fuego y Agua** (fuegoyagua.org) race in February, which has been gaining a reputation as an exciting challenge among runners. There are four races: a 100K, 50K, 25K, and Survival Run ($75-225). The courses go along the lakefront and up and over both volcanoes. The Survival Run includes a variety of tasks, like harvesting plantains and building your own raft. If you're visiting the island in February, book a room well in advance.

Santo Domingo

The most services for tourists are along the part of the beach in the town of Santo Domingo where lodging and restaurants are clustered together along the main road. The charming stone cabins at ★ **Villa Paraíso** (tel. 505/2563-4675, www.hotelvillaparaiso. com.ni, $35 private room, $75-92 cabin) feature air-conditioning, fridges, satellite TVs, and hot water. The breezy waterfront restaurant is fabulous, or order food to the shaded beachside pool. Call early for reservations as the place fills up quickly, especially on weekends and holidays.

A budget-friendly option is the beachfront **Buena Vista** ($25 d), a pleasant, family-run place offering plain rooms with clean sheets and fans. Farther down the road is **Hospedaje El Bosque** (tel. 505/2569-4871, $8 dorm, $15 s, $25 d), located next to the family's *pulpería* (small grocery store). The beach is just across the street.

San Fernando

Just outside Santo Domingo in San Fernando is **Hotel Xalli** (tel. 505/2569-4876, www.ometepebeachhotel.com, $45-111) with seven luxurious rooms all with hot water, TV, ceiling fan, air-conditioning, room service, and

Villa Paraíso

Wi-Fi. Enjoy the breeze in a hammock under the trees on the lakefront property.

Two kilometers farther down the beach toward Maderas is Santa Cruz. The first place you'll come to is the Sun Kite School (tel. 505/8287-5023, www.kiteboardingnicaragua. com, info@sunkiteschoool.com), just across the street from the beach. The instructors are certified by the International Kiteboarding Organization and have 15 years of teaching experience. Kayaks ($12/hour) are available. The owners also rent a sunny little room ($15-30) next to the kitchen with two beds and private bath that can fit up to three people. At the small, open-air Café de Paris (daily Nov.-July 8am-5pm, $3-6) out front, you'll find yummy French dishes like crepes and quiche.

★ Casa Hotel Istiám (just outside San Fernando, before Santa Cruz, tel. 505/2569-4879 or 505/8844-2200, casaistiam@hotmail. com, $8 pp shared bath, $10 pp private bath, $35 d with a/c and private bath) provides enormous value, and its beach is clean and pleasant. The rooms are so-so but affordable, and the location is spectacular, with an impressive view of both volcanoes from the second-floor deck. The service is friendly and the restaurant good. Make reservations in Moyogalpa at Hotel Ometepetl (across

from The Landing, half a block north of the dock on the right, tel. 505/2569-4276, ometepetlng@hotmail.com), as they sometimes fill up. Camping is also possible.

★ RÍO ISTIÁN

The paddle trip in a kayak or canoe up the Río Istián is best early in the morning or during sunset but is worthwhile at any time. You slip into the still waters of a marshy isthmus deep with shadow from the tree canopy and raucous with the sounds of birds, all under the reflection of two volcanic peaks.

The best place to base your trip from is Mérida, which is just three kilometers away by kayak. Edgard Lacayo at Aventuras en la Isla (tel. 505/8356-5108 or 505/8557-6251, $15-25) runs kayaking and wildlife tours from nearby El Perú, just 20 minutes from the river mouth. Caballito's Mar (5 km from Santa Cruz, turn right at the signs and follow the dirt road to the lake, tel. 505/8451-2093, www.caballitosmar.com, fernando@caballitosmar.com) rents kayaks by the hour and offers a fun three-hour guided trip ($20-25) in which they'll point out the kingfishers, white herons, turtles, and caimans. You can easily stay in their basic dormitory ($5 pp) or just have a meal (traditional Nicaraguan

kayak tour of the Río Isitián

and lots of lake fish, $3). You can also rent kayaks at Hacienda Mérida (tel. 505/2560-0496 or 505/8894-2551, www.hmerida.com) or Charco Verde (tel. 505/8887-9302 or 505/2560-1271, www.charcoverde.com.ni, charcoverde22@yahoo.es). Allow half a day for the adventure, and bring sunscreen, snacks, and plenty of water. During the dry season (Feb.-Apr.), some parts of the river may be too shallow for kayaking. During heavy rains in October, wind may be too fierce to make the trip. There's a short trail that starts in Playa Santo Domingo (behind Casa Hotel Istiám) that will allow you to see part of the marsh. The shorter paddle to Isla el Congo, just offshore, is nice as well, but beware the monkeys!

★ VOLCÁN MADERAS

Maderas is officially a national park, which will hopefully encourage preservation of the thick forests. Maderas is a pleasant volcano to climb, since the hike is in the shade, and is less demanding than its truly active twin. A guide is now obligatory since a pair of hikers got lost and eventually perished on the mountain. Even if you're not a peak bagger, there's lots to do here, starting with a guided visit to the fields of old petroglyphs behind

Finca Magdalena and Albergue Ecológico El Porvenir, a relic of the island's Nahuatl past. There is mountain biking down the rutted roads to take a coffee tour, horseback ride, or kayak trip. In addition, a host of unique places to stay (many based on working farms, some using permaculture and principles of environmental sustainability) are fun and interesting.

Santa Cruz and El Madroñal

Hostal Espirales (tel. 505/8355-2531, $8 dorm, $14 d with shared bath, $18 d private bath) is a two-minute walk from beach access.

Let the lapping waves of Lake Cocibolca rock you to sleep at Little Morgan's (tel. 505/8717-6475, www.littlemorgans.com, $10 tree house dorm beds, $20-35 private cabana), named after the charismatic Irish owner's young son. Chill to the satellite tunes, play a game of pool, or hang out in the rancho's lookout point. You'll find it on the main road, on the edge of Santa Cruz heading towards Balgüe. There is a restaurant (daily 7am-8pm) and a bar that stays open late (if you're a light sleeper best ask for a bed closer to the water).

Its location at the intersection of two main roads makes Rancho Santa Cruz (tel. 505/8884-9894, www.santacruzometepe.com, santacruzometepe@gmail.com, $1 hammock,

Volcán Maderas

$2 camping, $6 dorm, $10-20 private) an excellent base from which to explore in either direction, as your chances of catching a bus or taxi double. The restaurant (breakfast $2, lunch and dinner $4-6) serves granola, yogurt, and pancake breakfasts and a selection of vegetarian options including pastas and curries for lunch and dinner. You can rent bikes ($5/day), and they can arrange horseback riding on request.

The cabanas at Finca del Sol (tel. 505/8364-6394, $37-47), directly across the road from Little Morgan's, are small and homey. The whole place is sun-powered and eco-friendly, including the composting toilets, and the Finca is less mainstream. Chat with welcoming hosts Cristiano and Sheri over a home-cooked meal.

A 15-minute walk up the trail from the main road in El Madroñal leads to La Finca Ecológica El Zopilote (tel. 505/8369-0644 or 8961-8742, www.ometepezopilote.com, $3 to set up your tent, $4 hammock dorm, $12-20 private cabin), a hillside cluster of thatch huts and platforms run by some peace-loving Italians and their pack of hound dogs. Follow the well-placed signs. Check out the organic products in the gift shop (daily 10am-6pm) in the old bus by the road. They offer free yoga classes for guests (visitors pay $3). Pizza nights (Tues., Thurs., and Sat.) are a hit with guests.

Across the road is a small café called Jardín de Buhó (on Finca El Delirio, Mon.-Sat. 8am-9pm), owned by well-known Nicaraguan artist Juan Rivas and his wife, Marta. They make a great stir-fry, but you'll also find comida típica (local food) and some Chinese dishes. On Wednesdays and Fridays they have free movie nights (6:30pm). Their small hospedaje (200 meters behind the restaurant, tel. 505/2560-1460, jardindelbuho@ yahoo.com, $3 camping, $7 dorm, $15 private d with shared bath) is a short walk from a rocky lake beach. Marta is an anthropologist and offers archaeological tours ($5 each, minimum 5 people). The couple is interested in creating a shared artist space and is

the roadside gift shop at La Finca Ecológica El Zopilote

open to proposals from artists who want to share their skills with the surrounding local community.

Albergue Ecológico El Porvenir (tel. 505/2569-4420 or 505/2569-4426, doscarflores@yahoo.es, $10 pp private bath) is a peaceful hillside retreat with modern buildings, screened windows, volcano views, and lush tropical grounds. It's less ecological than it pretends, but you will nonetheless awaken to the sounds of the jungle. There is a one-hour trail to a lookout point with a great view of the isthmus and Concepción. If you're not a guest, you can visit for $1. It's a kilometer past Rancho Santa Cruz, and then 600 meters in from the sign on the road.

Balgüe

Balgüe is a convenient base for hiking Volcán Maderas. This pueblito has increasingly good lodging and food of its own. The stalwart of course is Finca Magdalena up on the skirts of the volcano itself, with petroglyphs and a compelling history, but various international

Finca Magdalena offers a great view of Volcán Concepción.

505/8811-3126 or 505/8216-9743, www.miti-erraometepe.com, $6 pp, $25 private room) in the town of Balgüe proper is a family-run *hospedaje* with 10 clean rooms. Fernando and his family can rent you a mountain bike ($7/day), a *moto* ($25/day), or a horse ($7/hr), and can easily arrange a volcano hike or transportation to all the local hot spots in their mini-bus. Down the next dirt road, The Lazy Crab (from the Catholic Church, 100 meters east, 20 meters toward the lake, tel. 505/5718-2191 or 505/8281-5303, $3 hammock, $6 dorm, $14 private room) is a new option run by a young local who's trying to promote sustainable tourism options in the community. He's got four clean rooms with mosquito nets and shared bath as well as a private room with a private bath. He also can organize a volcano hike and a farm tour with local INTUR-certified guides. Ask about kayak, horse, bike, and *moto* rental.

★ Finca Magdalena (tel. 505/8418-5636 or 505/8584-9298, www.fincamagdalena.com, $4 to string up a hammock or camp on the porch, $4 dorm cot, $6-22 private room, $43 private cabin, and more expensive cottages) is a 26-family working coffee cooperative established in 1983. The 195-year-old wooden house, once home to a plantation owner, tends towards austere, but its bare rooms have a romantic air of nostalgia, and the staff is welcoming and sincere. Coffee tours (1.5 hrs, $8 pp), petroglyph tours (1 hr, $6 pp), and guided hikes up to the lagoon atop Volcán Maderas are available. To get to Finca Magdalena, take the bus to Balgüe (get off at El Bamboo) and follow the signs along the 20-minute walk up the road to the farm (arrive before dark).

★ Casa del Bosque (from bus stop at El Bamboo, 1.5 km uphill from Bonafide's sign, tel. 505/8585-8933, $35-45 d) is a beautiful, secluded, three-bedroom house with spacious high-ceilinged rooms located on the Café Campestre farm, just below Bonafide. It's solar-powered with composting toilets and cool spring water showers, and has ample hangout space, including a BBQ area, large couch, and a porch with rocking chairs. The paths through the surrounding farm make for nice

newcomers (and a couple of locals) now provide a much greater range of options.

Check out the local women's co-op La Girasol (75 meters up the hill from El Bamboo, tel. 505/8365-2288, ask for Claudia, Mon. and Wed. 2pm-5pm), which has created jobs and income for a group of women in the community. They craft lovely coin purses, e-reader and laptop bags, cosmetic bags, and purses. Pick out your own fabric if you like. You can also buy their products at The Cornerhouse in Moyogalpa, which gives the cooperative 100 percent of the sale.

The best maintained bikes in Balgüe are at Danilo Ortiz's place across from the soccer field. If you're having trouble finding him, he's more commonly known by his nickname, Bro Chil (tel. 505/8402-2525, Mon.-Sat. 8am-5pm, $6/day).

ACCOMMODATIONS

If you'd like to get to know a local family in Balgüe, try a homestay.

If you're on a budget, Así Es Mi Tierra (tel.

The Petroglyphs of Ometepe

In the days of the Nahuatls, Volcán Maderas was called Coatlán, "the place where the sun lives," and Concepción was known as Choncoteciguatepe, "the brother of the moon," or Mestliltepe, "the peak that menstruates." In the lush forests of the lower slopes of the two volcanoes, the Nahuatls performed complicated rituals in honor of many different gods: Catligüe, the goddess of fertility; Ecatl, the god of air; Migtanteot, the god of death; Tlaloc, the god of soil; and Xochipillo, the goddess of happiness. The Nahuatl gods were all-powerful and vindictive, and spent their days in the land where the sun rises doing what all-powerful gods do best—feeding on human blood.

The concept of a soul was an important part of the Nahuatl belief system, as were the concepts of an afterlife and some form of reincarnation. Their calendar consisted of 18 months of 20 days each, for a total of a 360-day calendar year. They believed in a cycle of catastrophic events that recurred every 52 years. According to that cycle, the Nahuatls stored grains and water in preparation for that year.

Scattered around the island of Ometepe, but principally on the **north and northeastern slopes of Volcán Maderas** (behind Finca Magdalena, Albergue Ecológico El Porvenir, and Finca Ecológica El Zopilote), are the statues and petroglyphs, carved around the year AD 300, that paid homage to the Nahuatl gods. **Spirals** are a consistent theme, representing perhaps calendars or the Nahuatl concept of time and space. It has been suggested that spirals may also represent the islands themselves, or that the twin-spiral shape of Ometepe gave the island even more significance to the islanders, as it fit in with their ideas about the cosmos. More mundane images can also be identified in the carved rocks: monkeys, humans hunting deer, and a couple in coitus, suggesting Nahuatl wishes for prosperity and fertility, or just a bit of monkey business.

walks during the day. The owner lives in a cabin on the property—far enough to be private, but close enough to find if needed. The town is not far and bikes are available for guest use. You can order food from Café Campestre if you don't feel like making the trek yourself. Breakfast is served B&B style on-site in the kitchen, which is otherwise open for guest use. Ask about renting out the whole house.

FOOD
Chepito's Comedor (across from Café Campestre, Mon.-Sat. 8am-8pm, $3-5) offers quality Nica dishes at a reasonable price. **Big Lake** (down the side road where Lazy Crab is located, turn left at the lake, daily 9am-9pm, $3-10) has the best location in town, right on the lake with a shaded outdoor eating area and small dock jutting into the lake for swimming. Their specialty is fish, but they serve a variety of meals to please meat lovers and vegetarians alike. This is a picturesque spot to unwind at the end of the afternoon.

★ **Café Campestre** (in front of the Pentecostal church, daily 9am-8:30pm, $3-6)

has some of the best organic, farm-to-table food in Nicaragua. The menu offers mostly international fare; highlights include handmade pasta, hummus, dahl, okra, lasagna, and beer batter crepes. Don't miss house-roast coffee that's grown in Cajillas on the side of Maderas. The moonshine on the menu will make my fellow Kentuckians feel right at home.

Nisyros (farther down the road, on the right past the bus stop, daily 8am-11pm, $2-7) is run by an Italian man and his son. They serve a changing menu of Mediterranean cuisine, but you can always count on pizza and free Wi-Fi. Keep walking and you'll see Argentinean-owned **El Bamboo** (at the turnoff for Finca Magdalena, Mon.-Sat. 11am-10pm, $3-12). Their menu boasts big sandwiches on homemade bread, homemade ravioli, tofu, and sauces, smoothies, and local, organic coffee.

Mérida
It's still difficult to get out here, but Mérida is steadily increasing services to tourists. A rigorous and none-too-obvious trail leads to Maderas's crater lagoon from Mérida; you can

go down the way you came, or you can descend to the other side and emerge at Finca Magdalena or Finca Zopilote. But you absolutely must hire a guide, bring food and water, and get an early morning start: This is a serious hike for pros only.

Ride on horseback along the beach, through the forest, and beneath the full moon with **Hari's Horses** (300 meters east of El Pescadito, tel. 505/8383-8499, www.harishorses.com, harishorses@gmail.com, $10/hr), popular for his tours around the island on healthy, well-fed, trained animals.

ACCOMMODATIONS AND FOOD

Hari of Hari's Horses has bright, sunlit cabins at ★ **Finca Montaña Sagrada** ($45 d, includes yummy breakfast) with hot water and private decks complete with rocking chairs and amazing views.

★ **Hotel Hacienda Mérida** (tel. 505/2560-0496 or 505/8894-2551, www.hmerida.com, $5 camping, $8 dorm, $25-50 room with private bath, breakfast $5, dinner $7) is a friendly lakeside compound where second-floor balconies have views of the volcanoes and the lake. Take a swim from the private dock. They rent bikes and kayaks and can arrange hikes, fishing trips, tubing on the lake, and horseback riding ($5.50/hr); breakfast and dinner buffets are crafted with a nutrition focus from whole foods, many from the garden. Internet is available. The Nicaraguan owner, Alvaro Molina, speaks perfect English and is both a passionate advocate for and walking encyclopedia of Ometepe social causes. Ask about volunteer opportunities.

Farther down the road is ★ **Finca Mystica** (tel. 505/8751-9653 or 505/8119-1765, fincamystica.com, idigmud@gmail.com, $12 dorm, $35 private cabin), owned by a young U.S. family. Cabins are beautiful and made from organic materials. Their **Roots N Fruits Café** (daily 7:15am-8pm, $4-8) caters to all diets. Enjoy homemade raw chocolate, ginger beer, tasty baked goods, fresh bread and pizza from an earth oven, and locally grown house-roasted organic coffee.

Locally owned **Monkey's Island Hostel** (1 km south of Hacienda Mérida, tel. 505/8652-0971, $7 dorm, $12 shared bath, $20 private bath) has a friendly staff, boxy concrete rooms, and lousy feng shui. It's a short walk down some stairs to access the lake and sunset views.

San Ramón and Vicinity

Some 250 families fish and farm on Ometepe's least-visited shoreline, but it remains the "dark side of the moon": little visited but equally, if not more, compelling. Beyond San Ramón, the lonely east coast of Maderas is one of the most isolated spots in Nicaragua, connected tentatively by a poor excuse of a road with infrequent bus service. The locals are not used to receiving guests. It's potentially feasible to circumnavigate the entire volcano on foot or on a mountain bike (12 or 6 hours, respectively). The coast of Tichana hides lots of unexplored areas, including, reportedly, caves full of paintings as well as some petroglyphs near Corozal. There is one small *hospedaje* in San Ramón if you decide to stay the night. **Hospedaje La Cascada** (tel. 505/8573-3803 or 505/7847-6598, hospedajelacascadaometepe@gmail.com, $12 pp) is a five-room lakefront hostel with a small store and restaurant.

★ CASCADA SAN RAMÓN

It's a trek out to the isolated side of Maderas and then a two-hour hike uphill ($3 park entrance) to get to this waterfall, but it's well worth the effort. The signs say it is a three-kilometer trail, but it's likely more than that: allow three hours minimum, as a large portion of the trail is on an incline. Expect to get a little wet stomping through streams along the way. You can drive a four-wheel drive vehicle (or ride a horse) part way up to the water tank to skip past the exposed water pipes and head straight to the prettiest section of the hike. Otherwise, walk through avocado, mango, and lemon trees and up to a small parking area and hydroelectric plant. Once you enter the lush canyon, the humidity rises. You may have to scramble over some river rocks and at times the trail seems to disappear before it emerges a few meters ahead. At the waterfall you can bathe in an icy shallow pool and enjoy the view. You don't need a guide for this hike, but Hari's Horses (tel. 505/8383-8499, www.harishorses.com, harishorses@gmail.com) offers a popular horseback ride and guided hike to the waterfall ($40 pp) from Mérida. Having a local like Berman Gómez (tel. 505/8816-6971, ometepeisland@gmail.com) or one of the guides at UGO (tel. 505/8827-7714, ugometepe@yahoo.com) or Cacique Tours (tel. 505/8417-8692) to point out local wildlife along the way is invaluable.

MADERAS RAINFOREST CONSERVANCY

Four kilometers up the road from Merida, in the tiny village of San Ramón, the Maderas Rainforest Conservancy (formerly the Ometepe Biological Field Station, Miami tel. 305/666-9932, www.maderasrfc.org, info@maderasrfc.org) is a facility visited by student groups and researchers from all over the world. In addition to being active in numerous forward-thinking conservation projects in surrounding communities, MRC operates a field school on the volcano's slopes for undergraduate and graduate students in art and photography, primatology, ecology, bat ecology, botany, and other biological sciences. Tourists are welcome to sample the restaurant or stay at the station for a small fee.

GETTING THERE AND AWAY

Most visitors arrive by way of Rivas followed by a boat from San Jorge. Lake Cocibolca can get rough when the wind is high between November and February, at which times the larger boats are more comfortable. Avoid the roughest seas by traveling early morning and late evening, and sit near the center of the ferry where the rocking is slightest. The wind can sometimes contribute to ferries being cancelled altogether, so it's not a bad idea to plan a cushion of a day or two into your trip.

Cascada San Ramón

Boat from San Jorge

To access the dock, an employee of the municipal government will charge you $0.50. Boats from San Jorge on the mainland sail to Moyogalpa daily (1 hour). The trip offers great views of Omeptepe's towering volcanoes, and, barring rain, can be pleasant.

FERRY COMPANIES

The Ferry Ometepe I and III (tel. 505/8966-4978, $2.50) are big steel boats with radar and life jackets from whose roof you can travel in the fresh air. They depart San Jorge seven times daily 7:45am-5:45pm.

El Che Guevara (tel. 505/2563-0665 or 505/8694-1819, $2) runs from San Jorge to Moyogalpa at 7am and 4pm and departs Moyogalpa for San Jorge 11am and 5:30pm. A car and passenger ticket is $25, but make sure you reserve a spot in advance. Tickets can be purchased on board.

El Rey de Cocibolca (505/2552-8745, 505/8830-9995, 505/8691-3669 or 505/8833-4773, $2.50), a 1,300-passenger, four-story boat built in the Netherlands, plies the waters of Lake Nicaragua between San Jorge on the mainland and San José del Sur on Ometepe, a little town soon to become big thanks to the traffic. This boat departs from San José del Sur to the mainland at 7:30am and 3:20pm; from San Jorge to the island at 9:30am and 5pm. Bringing your vehicle costs less than $10 and the driver goes for free.

PRIVATE BOATS

The rest of the old San Jorge fleet provide a bumpier ride but are less expensive. These boats are independently owned and, unfortunately, rarely give honest information about the others; so if you're told, "The next boat doesn't leave for four hours," keep asking. Each company posts a sign with its own schedule; there is no main sign listing all the different times. UGO (office near the port in Moyogalpa, tel. 505/8827-7714) or Cacqiue Tours (kiosk in San Jorge port, tel. 505/8417-8692) will give you reliable information about the schedule.

From Moyogalpa to San Jorge, the *Karen María* leaves at 5:30am and 11:30am; the *Estrella del Sur* at 7am and 1pm; the *Santa Martha* at 6:30am and 3pm.

From San Jorge to Moyogalpa, the *Karen María* leaves at 9am and 1:30pm; the *Estrella del Sur* at 11am and 3:30pm; the *Santa Martha* at 12:30pm and 5pm.

From San José del Sur to San Jorge, the *Mozorola* leaves at 5:40am and returns from San Jorge at 2:30pm.

Boat from Granada and San Carlos

The Empresa Portuaria de Nicaragua (tel. 505/2552-2966 or 505/2552-4305) ferry leaves Granada on Mondays and Thursdays 2pm, arriving in Altagracia 6pm. The ship then continues onward to Morrito and San Miguelito on the southeastern lakeshore, arriving in San Carlos 5am.

On the return trip, the ferry leaves San Carlos on Tuesdays and Fridays 2pm, stops in Altagracia 11pm, and arrives in Granada at sunrise (4:30am). The price for a one-way passage between Granada and Ometepe is $9, but when seas are high, the ship will skip Ometepe altogether.

Air

Twice weekly flights land on the new landing strip several kilometers outside Moyogalpa on Thursdays and Sundays. Ometepe is part of the San Carlos–San Juan del Norte trip,

El Che Guevara ferry runs between San Jorge and Moyogalpa.

which means coming from Managua, the trip is short (20 min.), but the return is longer depending on where else passengers have booked flights. Book in advance with La Costeña (tel. 505/2298-5360, lacostena.online.com.ni). Flights depart Managua at noon and arrive at 3pm.

GETTING AROUND

Thanks to tourism, main roads have been paved and public transportation has improved on the island. You can take a slow public bus for under a buck, or you can catch a *colectivo* microbus. It's easiest to pay $20-35 for a taxi or private microbus to take you to the sites. If you're traveling with a cell phone and speak Spanish, it can be helpful to get your taxi driver's number so you can call later and make arrangements yourself.

You can also rent a motorcycle or scooter, or hitchhike. Once you've accommodated your stuff at your hotel, biking is an enjoyable, cheap, and relatively fast way to get around the island if you take it easy, drink plenty of water, and don't mind riding a clunker. Also try horseback riding, offered across the island, though there's no guarantee you'll get a well-trained, well-fed animal.

Bus

Buses are few and far between on Sundays, which remain a tough day to get around the island in anything but a rented vehicle, taxi, or by availing yourself of the services of your hotel.

In general, there's a bus in Moyogalpa to meet every boat. For the most up-to-date schedule, ask around the dock, or stop in the UGO office (north end of the port, tel. 505/8827-7714). A bus leaves for the town of Altagracia every hour 4:30am-7pm. Fully 90 percent of the buses leave the Moyogalpa dock, travel straight up the hill along the main street, stop at the park, then head east out of town on the road to Altagracia (passing through San José del Sur); the other 10 percent turn left, passing through La Flor and San Marcos on their way to Altagracia, which takes longer due to the rough road.

From Altagracia, buses depart for Playa Santo Domingo every hour on the hour. From Moyogalpa to Santo Domingo there are buses six times daily 8:20am-4:40pm. A bus passes through from Santo Domingo in the other direction 12 times daily 4:30am-5pm, but the schedule is sporadic.

Three daily buses depart for Balgüe from the dock in Moyogalpa, at 8:20am, 10:20am,

See Ometepe on horseback.

and 3:45pm, taking nearly two hours. Return buses leave for Moyogalpa at 5:30am and 1:30pm. Three daily buses leave Moyogalpa for Mérida at 8:30am, 2:40pm, and 4:30pm; from Altagracia buses depart at 7am, 10:30am, and 2pm (these buses continue to San Ramón, returning the following day starting at 5:30am). From Mérida to Moyogalpa, buses leave at 4am, 8:30am, and 3:30pm. If you board a bus in Moyogalpa that's heading to Maderas, remember you'll pass through Altagracia first. From Moyogalpa to Altagracia, it's approximately one hour, and from Altagracia to Balgüe it's about a half hour. The island is bigger than you think.

There is no direct public transportation between Balgüe and San Ramón, so you have to take a bus to *el cruce* at Santa Cruz and then catch a bus down the other road, depending on the direction you're going.

Car

Drivers should take care with the rocky and unfamiliar terrain. It's easy to damage your rental on Ometepe's back roads. There are no rental agencies on the island. Arrange a transfer with your hotel or a tour operator beforehand. Most hotels will gladly help to arrange tours as well, getting you up the volcanoes or on waterfall hikes, horseback rides, kayaking excursions, and other area attractions.

Rivas

Rivas is a languorous colonial town of traders and farmers. Hundreds of thousands of passengers traveling between New York and California passed through its streets in horse-drawn carts between San Jorge and San Juan del Sur; this was the only dry-land crossing of the entire gold rush journey. At about the same time, one of filibuster William Walker's first military defeats took place here. Nowadays Rivas is southern Nicaragua's most important city, a commercial center whose small population (under 50,000) helps it retain an old-world charm. Few travelers visit Rivas as a destination proper, but it remains an important companion town for San Juan del Sur and Ometepe, providing a better selection of medical, banking, and shopping services. Don't discount it as inconsequential: It's one of Nicaragua's more pleasant cities, charismatic and enjoyable in its own right, and has historical sites worth visiting.

Rivas is often hot because of its low altitude, but a cool lake breeze from Lake Cocibolca makes it bearable. Rivas is known as Ciudad de los Mangos due to the abundance of the trees in and around the city. swarms of chatty *chocoyos* (parakeets) feast on the fruit, their calls filling the skies around sunset.

SIGHTS

Rivas is the birthplace of several presidents of the republic, most recently, Violeta Barrios de Chamorro (Coalition, governed 1990-1997). Chamorro's childhood home is located across the street from the Iglesia Parroquial de San Pedro's south side. The modest Emmanuel Mongalo y Rubio Monument marks the final resting place of a local schoolteacher and hero who lived here in the mid-1800s. His actions during the Battle of Rivas resulted in the capture of William Walker.

Iglesia Parroquial de San Pedro

Rivas's obvious centerpiece is a well-loved historical monument repainted in 2007. Built in the 18th century, the Iglesia Parroquial de San Pedro (mass: Mon.-Fri. 7am and 5pm, Sat. 7am, Sun. 8:30am, 11:30am, and 5:30pm) has witnessed the California gold rush, William Walker, the Sandinista Revolution, and the 21st-century real estate boom. As you take in the details of the church's pleasing colonial design, remember that every single gold rush-bound passenger that traversed Nicaragua in the days of Cornelius

Rivas

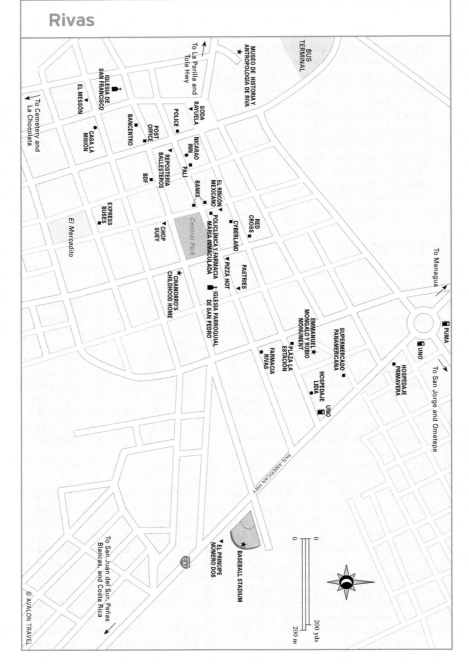

BUS TERMINAL

MUSEO DE HISTORIA Y
ANTROPOLOGIA DE RIVA

To La Parilla and
Tola Hwy

IGLESIA DE
SAN FRANCISCO

EL MESSON

To Cemetery and
La Chocolata

SODA
RAFUELA

POLICE

NICARAO
INN

POST
OFFICE

BANCENTRO

CASA LA
MISION

REPOSTERIA
BALLESTEROS

PALI

BDF

EXPRESS
BUSES

BANKS

El Mercadito

EL RINCON
MEXICANO

Central Park

CYBERLAND

CHOP
SUEY

POLICLINICA Y FARMACIA
MARIA INMACULADA

CHAMORRO'S
CHILDHOOD HOME

RED
CROSS

PIZZA HOT

PASTRIES

IGLESIA PARROQUIAL
DE SAN PEDRO

To Managua

EMMANUEL
MONGALO Y RUBIO
MONUMENT

SUPERMERCADO
PANAMERICANA

PLAZA LA
ESTACIÓN

FARMACIA
RIVAS

HOSPEDAJE
LIDIA

UNO

PUMA

UNO

HOSPEDAJE
PRIMAVERA

To San Jorge and Ometepe

PAN-AMERICAN HWY

To San Juan del Sur, Peñas
Blancas, and Costa Rica

EL PRINCIPE
NÚMERO DOS

BASEBALL STADIUM

0

0

200 yds

200 m

© AVALON TRAVEL

Vanderbilt's steamship line passed under its shadow. It is today, as always, a peaceful place to seek refuge. At the time of research the church's interior was being remodeled and only open for Sunday service. The rest of the week mass is held in the small chapel at the back of the church.

Iglesia de San Francisco

Four blocks west of the park at the town's center, the Iglesia de San Francisco was built in 1778 and was the first convent of the Franciscan friars. A beautiful statue commemorates the devotion of the friars to both God and their work. When construction of the nearby Bancentro began, an underground tunnel was discovered that linked the Iglesia de San Francisco with the plaza (the open area adjacent to the central park's north side); the tunnel passes beneath the old school (now a ruin one door east of Bancentro). Researchers speculate it was probably dug at the same time as the church, meaning it was in place and probably used during the Battle of Rivas, when the plaza was the site of a military barracks.

Museo de Historia y Antropología de Rivas

Rivas has its own history museum: the Museo de Historia y Antropología de Rivas (on the western side of town, tel. 505/2534-2129, Mon.-Fri. 8am-noon and 2pm-5pm, Sat. only in the morning, foreign travelers $2), in a 200-year-old house that was once part of a cacao and indigo plantation. Once known as the Casa Hacienda Santa Úrsula, on June 29, 1855, William Walker and his men were defeated here in a heroic battle that Nicaraguans are still proud of. The Battle of Rivas, as it became known, was one of the first manifestations of Nicaragua's growing sense of independence in the late 19th century. In fact, the people of Rivas claim "nationalism began in Rivas." The museum has a healthy collection of pre-Columbian pottery; domestic utensils from the 18th and 19th centuries including kerosene lamps, silverware, and hand tools; and several old maps of the region. The building itself evokes the lifestyle of the old farming community. The hours of operation are more of a suggestion than a rule, so stop by and try your luck.

ENTERTAINMENT AND EVENTS

El Principe Número Dos (next to the baseball stadium on the highway) is a popular bar, especially on Saturdays, and the restaurant is a

Iglesia Parroquial de San Pedro

staple among locals. Chuperman (new Plaza La Estación, 1.5 blocks west of the old Texaco, daily 3pm-midnight) and El Nambaro (new Plaza La Estación, 1.5 blocks west of the old Texaco, daily 2pm-midnight) are nearly identical smaller bars with shaded outdoor seating. A bit more interesting, though slightly seedy, is El Rincón Mexicano (1 block north of BanPro, daily 10am-10pm), which serves Nicaraguan versions of Mexican dishes, along with lots of beer. You're sure to be the only foreigner in the bar.

No one enjoys baseball as much as the people of Rivas. At last count, there were 138 officially registered baseball teams and more than 3,900 registered players in the municipality, with stadiums or makeshift diamonds in every village in the department! Attending a Sunday afternoon game ($1) in Rivas's main stadium on the highway is a great way to experience the city and the energy of its people. In lieu of chilidogs, there's plenty of *vigorón* (fried pork and yucca) and enchiladas in the grandstand.

ACCOMMODATIONS

Few travelers find a reason to spend the night in Rivas, and the Ometepe-bound tend to prefer the lakeside places in San Jorge. But if you're planning to catch an early bus on the highway, there's no reason not to spend the night. For budget travelers, ★ Hospedaje Lidia (half a block west of the old Texaco station, tel. 505/2563-3477, $10 pp shared bath, $12 private bath) is the most popular and has a dozen clean rooms situated around a pretty little garden, including large rooms for up to five people (groups ask about discounts). From here it's an easy walk to the highway to catch a bus north or south.

Hospedaje Hilmor (behind the Iglesia Parroquial de San Pedro, tel. 505/2830-8175, $6 s, $12 d with shared bath, $12 s, $18 d with private bath) is an option, though not quite as nice as Hospedaje Lidia. Hospedaje Primavera (next to the Shell station, $5 pp private bath) is a bare-bones lodge catering mostly to working Nicaraguan expats on their way to and from Costa Rica.

The Nicarao Inn (a block west of the park, tel. 505/2563-3234, www.hotelnicarao-inn.com.ni, $40 s, $50 d, includes breakfast) is efficient and modern with cable TV, air-conditioning, Wi-Fi, a guarded parking lot, pleasant lobby, and attentive staff. At the inn, you can arrange rides to San Juan del Sur and other parts. ★ Casa La Misión (southeastern corner of the Iglesia de San Francisco, tel. 505/2563-0384, $35-50) has character and large bathrooms, but no hot water. The highlight is the lovely, vine-covered, stonewall patio where you can enjoy your breakfast.

FOOD

Buy fresh pastries and juice at Repostería Don Marcos (a block east of the park), an easy breakfast en route between San Juan del Sur and the boat to Ometepe. If you've got some time, the outdoor seating at Repostería Ballesteros (across from the Nicarao Inn) lends itself to quality people-watching. Their pastries are a nationwide sensation.

Possibly the lowest-price lunch in town is Soda Rayuela (north side of the police station, daily 7am-8pm, $2-8), serving simple sandwiches, chicken, and burgers. Get your pizza fix at Pizza Hot (across the street from the Iglesia Parroquial de San Pedro, closed Mon.). Enjoy a slice at one of their outdoor tables. In the evening, street-side *fritangas* are plentiful. The dishes at Chop Suey (southwest corner of the park, daily 10am-9pm, $5-7 per plate), a Chinese place not far off the mark, have been subtly adapted to suit the Nicaraguan palate. El Messón (south side of Iglesia de San Francisco, tel. 505/2563-4535, daily 11am-2:30pm), serves a decent Nicaraguan buffet lunch as well as *caballo bayo*, a hearty stew.

★ La Parilla (1 block west of the historic museum, tel. 505/2563-1700, daily 11am-midnight, $5-10) is a nice option with outdoor seating preferred by locals for watching baseball games on TV. This is top-quality Nicaraguan food; you can't go wrong with anything off the grill. They serve the fanciest *tostones con queso* (fried plantains with cheese), with salad stuffed into cup-shaped fried plantains atop a thin layer of *frijoles molidos* (refried beans). El Mariscazo (800 meters south of the baseball stadium, tel. 505/2563-1077, daily 10am-9pm) is a popular seafood restaurant on the highway. Splurge on the grilled lobster.

INFORMATION AND SERVICES

Several well-stocked pharmacies in town make Rivas a good service stop for the San Juan del Sur beach crowd. Policlínica y Farmacia María Inmaculada (north side of the central park, tel. 505/2563-4935, Mon.-Sat. 7am-8pm, Sun. 8:30am-12:30pm and 4:30pm-7:30pm) is a pharmacy and private clinic providing doctors of various specialties (consultation Mon.-Fri. 8am-5pm, Sat. 8am-noon). Another well-stocked pharmacy is the Farmacia Rivas (2.5 blocks east of the park at the intersection of the boulevard, tel. 505/2563-4292). For more serious issues, the Hospital Gaspar García Laviana (tel. 505/2563-3301) is located on the Tola highway.

There are several banks in town including BDF, Bancentro, Banpro, and BAC, all of which operate Monday-Friday 8:30am-4:30pm, Saturday 8:30am-noon. Most are located on the main road near the central park. Internet cafés are easy to find around the city.

The Costa Rican Consulate in Rivas was temporarily closed at the time of research. The police station (tel. 505/2563-3732, rivas@policia.gob.ni) is two blocks west of the central park.

GETTING THERE AND AWAY

Buses leave Managua's Roberto Huembes terminal for Rivas every 30 minutes. Several express buses depart before 8am. Express buses to San Juan del Sur and the border at Peñas Blancas will let you off on the highway at Rivas. They leave Huembes at 5am, 8am, 9:30am, and 3:30pm. While you can catch a bus easily on the highway, often these are standing room only. If you want a better chance at getting a seat on an express bus to Managua, get a *triciclo* to El Mercadito.

A good way to reach Jinotepe, Masaya, Carazo, and the Pueblos Blancos is to take one of the express minibuses, which leave from El Mercadito on the south end of town about once every hour ($2.50). Regular buses leave from the market on the northwest side of Rivas: every hour for Jinotepe and Granada; every 25 minutes for Nandaime, Masaya, and Managua. The last bus for Managua leaves from the old Texaco station on the highway at 6pm. Four daily buses go to Belén and six to Las Salinas (9am-4:30pm).

To Costa Rica

Bus service to Peñas Blancas and the border (less than an hour, every 30-45 minutes, less than $1) runs 5am-5:30pm. You can also share a *colectivo*. On the highway there's a Tica Bus office (150 meters north of old Texaco station, tel. 505/8453-2228) in Pulpería la Diamante where you can buy tickets north or south. The bus passes by Rivas each morning bound for Costa Rica between 7am and 8am, and between 3pm and 4pm every afternoon bound for Managua. Buy your tickets ($29 to San José, Costa Rica) the day before.

Taxi to San Jorge and San Juan del Sur

To San Jorge and the ferry to Ometepe, a taxi should cost you no more than $1 per person, whether you take it from the highway traffic circle or from Rivas proper. Ignore any taxi driver that tries to charge $2 or more, unless you're traveling after 10pm, when taxi prices go up. Taxis from Rivas to San Juan del Sur cost around $25, or $2 if it's a *colectivo*, which only run during daylight hours.

GETTING AROUND

A common landmark used in Rivas addresses is the old Texaco station *(la antigua Texaco)*, which is now one of two Uno stations. Rivas is full of *triciclo* bike taxis eager for clients. These are known locally as *pepanos* after the first man in Rivas to ever use one (*"pepano"* was his nickname). You can catch a ride in one for about $0.60. Many taxi drivers prefer to work longer distances, as opposed to locally, but you can hail one to take you across town for under $1.

NANDAIME

Just south of where the highways from Granada and Carazo join to continue on to Rivas and the border, you'll pass by the mid-size city of Nandaime, located on the Pan-American Highway in the shadow of Volcán Mombacho. This is a humble, unassuming pueblo with the most basic of traveler's amenities, a small-town tranquility, and a passion for music. Nandaime's most famous son is Camilo Zapata, a key founder of the Nicaraguan folk style, who composed the song, "El Nandaimeño." Nandaime is also home to three *chichera* groups, ragtag bands composed of a bass drum, a snare, cymbals, a sousaphone, and loud, clashing brass. Known as "orchestras," they participate frequently in parades and bullrings, and their music is happy, loud, and scrappy.

On the southern side of the Mombacho volcano is a rural community tourism project, **Aguas Agrias** (tel. 505/2552-0238 or 505/8896-9361, turismo@ucatierrayagua. org), so-named for its lime-flavored waters. Local guides offer two-hour hikes ($3 pp) pointing out local wildlife, crops, and wonderful views of the volcano, ending at the Manares River for a swim in its natural clear waters sourced from beneath the volcano. Or, take a four-hour hike ($5 pp) to the hidden Laguna Verde, one of the lagoons of Mecatepe. Order a meal from the communal house before you leave, so it's ready on your return. Aguas Agrias lies 12 kilometers from the community of Monte Verde (located between Granada and Nandaime). If you're arriving via public transport, tell the *cobrador* to let you off at Monte Verde. From there you can take a moto-taxi ($4-5). You can also arrange private transport through UCA Tierra y Agua.

SAN JORGE

A traditional village with a strong Catholic spirit, San Jorge is primarily a port town and farming community that produces plantains. Nearby **Popoyuapa,** true to its Nahuatl-sounding name, cultivates cacao, the tree whose seed is used to produce cocoa and eventually chocolate, and which was once used by the Nicarao people as a form of currency.

The tiny lakeside port of San Jorge is your access point to La Isla de Ometepe and as such, most travelers breeze straight through it on the way to catch a boat. If you have an hour to kill before your ferry departs, there's no reason to spend it dockside sitting on your luggage. Some travelers find San Jorge a pleasant place to spend a night, and the locals are turning out increasingly acceptable hotel accommodations (mostly targeting the backpacker set). The port expansion was underway at the time of research, but it is expected to include a park and several kiosks, which will house tour operators and food vendors.

Be advised that at certain unpredictable times of the year, a southern wind brings plagues of *chayules,* small white gnats that swarm the lakeside in San Jorge and eastern shores of Ometepe. They neither bite nor sting but are relentless and always seem to wind up in your mouth.

Sights

Halfway down the long road to town, you'll pass under **La Cruz de España,** a graceful concrete arch that suspends a stone cross directly over San Jorge's main drag. This main street runs through town down to the water's edge and the docks. The monument commemorates—and is ostensibly built over the very place where—on October 12, 1523, Spanish conquistador Gil González Dávila and indigenous cacique Nicarao-Calli first met and exchanged words.

Across the street from the base of the arch is a **mural** commemorating the same event, with the words attributed to Nicarao: "The Spanish know about the flood, who moved the stars, the sun, and the moon. Where the soul was found. How Jesus, a man, is God and his virgin mother giving birth, and why so few men wanted so much gold." Many believe that the Spanish went on to refer to Nicaragua as The Land of Nicarao, which over time evolved into the modern word Nicaragua.

The squat Iglesia de las Mercedes is one of Central America's earliest churches. Built around the year 1575, it was renovated and re-painted a bright yellow in 2001. San Jorge's kilometer-long beach is hugely popular among Nicaraguans, who flock there during Semana Santa to enjoy the lake and the awesome view of twin-peaked Ometepe on the horizon.

Entertainment and Events

San Jorge celebrates its *fiestas patronales* annually April 19-23 (the date changes to ac-commodate Semana Santa when necessary), at which time you can expect the beach to be packed. San Jorge usually has a parade during the celebrations, and there are performances of traditional dances, including Las Yeguitas (The Dance of the Little Mares) and Los Enmascarados (The Dance of the Masked Ones). Neighbors in Rivas prefer this celebra-tion to their own patron saint celebrations.

Accommodations and Food

If you missed the last boat to La Isla and don't feel like backtracking to Rivas, book one of the rooms at Hotel Hamacas (less than 100 meters west of the dock tel. 505/2563-0048 or 505/8810-4144, hotelhamacas.com, $32 d with private bath and fan, $42 with a/c, includes breakfast).

You won't go hungry in San Jorge's nu-merous food-and-drink joints lining the beachfront, but neither will you be surprised by the menu: chicken, beef, fish, fries, burg-ers, and sandwiches. Near the dock entrance, expect to find higher prices aimed at tour-ists. Try the mazorcas de cacao stand (250 meters west of the dock, in front of the school), where you'll find a sweet of cacao mixed with sugar, cinnamon, pepper, and cloves unique to this region. Italian-owned Bar y Restaurante El Navegante (next to the dock, tel. 505/8601-1762, Wed.-Mon. 11am-8:30 pm, $4-10) is a decent place to wait for the ferry and enjoy the lakeside view. The menu has sandwiches, pastas, and a va-riety of delicious seafood options including salmon and snapper. Sol y Arena (north of the dock, $5-20) offers pizzas, pastas, and burgers.

Getting There

A taxi from Granada straight to the dock in San Jorge is about $30. From Managua, take any southbound bus from the Huembes bus terminal to Rivas and get off at the traffic circle on the highway. From the traffic circle in Rivas to the dock at San Jorge is four ki-lometers, accessible by Rivas buses once an hour ($0.25); they pass the traffic circle ap-proximately 20 minutes after the hour. If you don't happen to be there at that right moment, take a *colectivo* taxi to San Jorge ($1 pp; ignore anyone who tries charging more). (It may be easier to do this once you've left behind the crowd of taxi drivers who bombard passengers getting off the bus.) There is one Managua-San Jorge express, departing Huembes at 9am, arriving in San Jorge at 10:50am. The same bus departs San Jorge at 5pm, arriving in Managua at 6:50pm.

San Juan del Sur

This beach town has been changing and developing rapidly over the past few years and is really starting to give Granada a run for its money. With the construction of the town's new marina, locals expect cruise lines to bring herds of new visitors. Even so, when the waves die down and tourism slows, quite a few places close up shop (Sept.-Oct.).

The main show in town is the brightly colored day's end over the languid harbor waves. San Juan sunsets can go on for hours; make sure you're on the beach as the setting sun drapes the fishing boats in shadow and the rock face of El Indio dims behind the evening. San Juan del Sur's crescent-shaped beach washed with the gentle, warm waves of the protected harbor have been attracting travelers for a long time. In the 1850s, this quiet fishing village experienced its first brief boom as a transport hub for gold rush pioneers crossing the peninsula on Cornelius Vanderbilt's passenger route to California. This was also where many of William Walker's glory-seeking soldiers disembarked to join his ill-fated adventure. After the gold rush, the town sank into obscurity and tropical lethargy, where it remained for a century-and-a-half.

At the turn of the 21st century, San Juan del Sur again grew in international popularity to the steady drumbeat of high-profile international press coverage declaring the area a real estate hot spot. The area attracted a frenzy of property pimps, land sharks, and a flock of checkbook-toting prospectors scouring the coastline for a piece of the pie. The economic growth was not without scuffles, and there is still some tension, but some of the investment led to progress, new establishments, and healthy relationships between foreign investors determined to make money *and* a positive impact for their Nicaraguan colleagues.

SAFETY

San Juan del Sur is a nice town, but as tourists and foreigners increasingly populate it, thieves come out of the woodwork. Here are a couple of tips from the locals: avoid the beach after dark; keep your wits about you when walking around late at night. There's a

port in San Juan del Sur

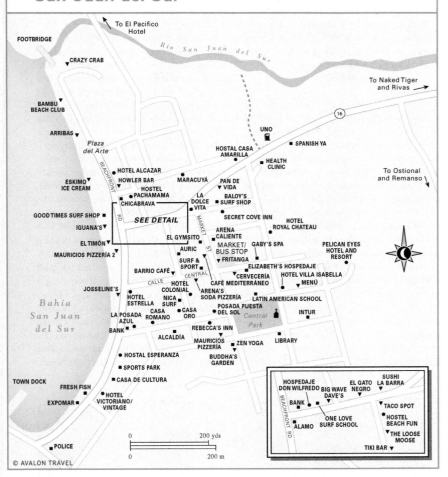

San Juan del Sur

nice quiet spot in the rocks on the north end of the beach for watching the sunset but it has a reputation for robberies. If your car is parked in town, be sure it's locked and valuables are stowed. Holdups sometimes occur on the roads to nearby beaches. A common tactic is to put some sort of obstacle across the road that the driver has to get out and move. There's no reason to stress about safety in San Juan del Sur, just be smart.

ENTERTAINMENT AND EVENTS

The community-run Casa de Cultura (on the main beach drag, tel. 505/8450-8990) offers classes to foreigners and locals. Most popular are dance lessons ($5 pp)—pick from salsa, merengue, *bachata,* or local *folklórico.* (Check out their *folklórico* presentation on Thursday evenings at El Timón.) They also offer free art classes for kids.

San Juan del Sur's mellow, year-round party scene picks up around Christmas, New Year's Eve, and Semana Santa when the town is flooded with visitors. Managuan club owners set up beach discos during the high season. Places come and go quickly, and it can be difficult to keep up with what's open.

Nightlife

An old favorite is the Crazy Crab (at the north end of the beach, 300 meters north of El Timón, daily 8am-5pm), popular for after-hours dancing on weekends. If you make it 'til 5am, you get a free *nacatamal*. Instead of walking, take a taxi home at night. Another San Juan del Sur classic is Iguana's (on the beach road, 50 meters west of the BAC, tel. 505/8635-5204, www.iguanabeachbar.com), which caters to locals and foreigners alike— Matthew McConaughey even showed up here once. The upper level deck heats up late night. El Timón (next door to Iguana's, 50 meters west of the BAC) offers a classier atmosphere and great happy hour prices (4pm-6pm). A bit farther down the strip is another enjoyable waterfront bar, Arribas (300 meters north of El Timón), an after-hours bar with a more chill vibe; things pick up after midnight. Open all day, Big Wave Dave's (25 meters

east of El Timón, daily 7:30am-10pm) is another fixture in San Juan's bar scene with a Margaritaville vibe. Check out live Blues night on Wednesdays.

As expats increasingly flock to this beach town, a plethora of exciting new options have cropped up in recent years. Many of these bars host theme nights like karaoke and trivia. Howler Bar (half a block north of Iguana's on the beach road, 100 meters north of El Timón, daily 10am-2am) is a popular new favorite. San Juan del Sur Cervecería (half a block east of the market, sjdsbrewers.com, sjdsbrewers@gmail.com, from 4pm daily) is one of the only places in the country where you can find a microbrew. Expect IPAs, wheat beers, and more creative options like Passion Fruit Ale. They give brewery tours (5:30pm, $15 pp). At Canadian-owned The Loose Moose (50 meters south of El Gato Negro, tel. 505/8255-6395) you can enjoy poutine and Caesars (a Canadian cocktail similar to a Bloody Mary) while watching a hockey game. It's a small place and fills up quickly. Farther down this road is Tiki Bar (from the market, 1 block west, half a block north, Mon.-Sat. 11am-11pm), where you can try a Tiki Bomb (coconut water and a shot of rum) served in the style of a Jaeger Bomb.

church in San Juan del Sur's central park

Belgian-owned Rebublika (one block west of the market, tel. 505/8282-7935, daily 8:30am-midnight) has a huge drink selection, BBQ, and trivia nights.

Festivals and Events

Sunday Funday (from 2:30pm, $30 pp) is one of the newer developments in the party scene and is popular among tourists but not among locals (for the debauchery that often ensues). It's a pool bar crawl starting at Pelican Eyes (on the hill above town, tel. 505/2563-7000, www.pelicaneyesresort.com), then moving to Naked Tiger (Km 138 on the highway outside of town, tel. 505/8621-4738, www.thenakedtigerhostel.com), and ending at Hostel Pachamama (from El Gato Negro, 2 blocks south, tel. 505/2568-2043, www.hostelpachamama.com, guests pay half price). Sign up at one of these three places the morning of. Fight Night (oxeventsfightnight. com, $11.50) runs four times throughout the year. Watch well-matched pros and amateurs, who train at the Gimnacio (a block east of the Catholic church), duke it out for local glory and bragging rights. Find the schedule on their website. Every March, expats organize the Earthship Pitaya Festival (earthship-pitayafestival.com), a weekend of parties, concerts, and a surf competition.

San Juan del Sur's *fiestas patronales* are June 16-24, with bull riding, pole climbing, greased pig catching, and Coca-Cola chugging contests, followed by Procesión de la Virgen del Carmen on July 17. Locals parade the icon, the Patron Saint of Fishermen, through town and to the docks where waiting boats take her (and as many locals as possible) for a lap around the bay. On September 2 the town commemorates the tidal wave of 1992, a 62-foot monster that swept across Main Street, destroying many structures (and farther up the coast, entire villages, like El Tránsito).

San Juan del Sur has their own version of Ahüizotes (a copycat of the popular Masaya festival) on October 24 in which people dress as popular Nicaraguan myths and legends and parade through the streets at night. CANTUR organizes the Aperatura del Verano every weekend for four weeks leading up to Semana Santa. It includes concerts, *carnaval*-style parades, folkloric dance presentations, and a beach volleyball competition.

SHOPPING

During weekends, holidays, and cruise ship arrivals, street vendors from Masaya and as far as Guatemala and Argentina can be found in the Plaza del Arte (on the road in front of the beach). Most everyday items, including fresh vegetables and those dollar flip-flops you've been looking for, can be purchased in or around the Municipal Market (center of town, daily 7am-7pm). On Saturdays an organic farmer's market (7:30am-1pm) sets up in Big Wave Dave's.

There are some trendy surf shops popping up around town. SanJuanSurf (www.san-juansurf.com) is a clothing line, sold at many local shops, run by Englishman Sean Dennis, who came eight years ago to surf, and never left. The clothing is handmade and designed in Nicaragua with profits donated to worthy causes. ChicaBrava (1.5 blocks north of El Timón, U.S. tel. 713/893-5261) stocks well-known clothing brands at their oceanfront store. Auric (from Barrio Café, 50 meters north, www.auricsurf.com, daily 9am-7pm, closes early on Sun.) sources their clothing from women-run Nicaraguan businesses, and the clothing is hand-finished locally. If you forgot your surf bikini, Santosha Organic (in front of Hotel Estrella, facing the beach, tel. 505/8458-1816, daily 10am-8pm) has got you covered. They also sell a variety of Nicaraguan-made artisan products, including chocolate, honey, coffee, and jam. They've started their own clothing line, Santosha Couture, and they sell Olibobolly dolls (olibobolly.com), which are locally made by Nicaraguan women. Your purchase pays for a second doll that is donated to a Nicaraguan child.

RECREATION

The Sports Park (next to the Casa de Cultura on the main beach drag) has volleyball and soccer facilities with league games on weeknights. During the rest of the day, the park is open for (often competitive) pickup games. Otherwise, expect soccer games to be played on the hard sand beach at low tide on either end of the bay.

★ Surfing

Most surfers make base camp in San Juan del Sur and then drive or boat out to the better breaks, though a lot of beaches are now also developing accommodations of their own. Many of the best breaks are only accessible by boat. There are plenty of hostels, tour operators, and surf shops that run daily shuttles to the nearest beaches: Maderas, Hermosa, Remanso, Yanqui, and Marsella.

An adequate selection of new and used surfboards is easy to find in San Juan. Local shredders Byron and Kervin López can be found in their shop, Arena Caliente (next to the market, tel. 505/8815-3247, www.arena-caliente.com). They'll rent you a board, drive you out to the beach, and teach you the basics for $32. Baloy's Surf Shop (a block east of El Gato Negro) is owned by another pair of Nicaraguan brothers who learned to surf on a secondhand board left behind by a tourist. They can arrange boards, gear, transportation, and lessons. Run by surfboard shaper Tom Eberly, Nica Surf (tel. 505/8934-3669, U.S. 760/473-9529, www.nicasurfinterna-tional.com, info@nicasurfinternational.com) provides similar services and sells Eberly's namesake boards out of the local store.

Good Times Surf Shop (next to Iguana's, tel. 505/8675-1621, www.goodtimessurfshop.com, board rental $10/day) rents boards and sells new and used boards. They can help you arrange for ding repair, or head to Mosco Repair (outside Barrio Café), known for speed and quality. Good Times also offers trips to local surf breaks starting at $10 per person. One Love Surf School (next to Don Wildfredo's, tel. 505/8251-5525) offers two-hour classes for $30 daily. Beach shuttles are $5 and surf tours are $15.

ChicaBrava (tel. 505/8894-2842, www.chicabrava.com) is the first all-women's surf camp in Nicaragua, with high-end, all-inclusive packages that cover lodging, food, equipment, six days of instruction, and transportation. You can also stay at their flagship "cloud farm" nature retreat with many activities available, including a catamaran cruise.

surfing in San Juan del Sur

Sailing and Diving

The Pacific lacks the visibility of the Caribbean waters, but fish are plentiful and there's a sunken Russian shrimp boat offshore, so diving can be fun. The expert divers at San Juan's Nicaraguan-owned and -operated dive shop, **Neptune Watersports** (tel. 505/2568-2752 or 505/8903-1122, www. neptunenicadiving.com, $85 for two tanks, $350 for open-water certification), will rent you gear and take you underwater if you already have your license and are an experienced diver.

San Juan Surf & Sport (20 meters west of the market, tel. 505/8984-2464, sanjuandelsursurf.com, sanjuandelsurs_s@yahoo.com) offers tours and can take you fishing. Dario and his laid-back crew provide the equipment and will show you how to cast; you can keep any fish you catch. They have a new tour to the calm and remote Playa Blanca ($35 pp) that includes fishing, snorkeling, beer, and lunch.

SUNSET CRUISE

San Juan Surf & Sport (20 meters west of the market, tel. 505/8984-2464, sanjuandelsursurf.com, sanjuandelsurs_s@yahoo. com, $23 pp) offers a daily sunset cruise in a fancy *panga*. Expect great photo ops, a merry crowd, and an open bar. **Nica Sail n' Surf** (tel. 505/8980-1213, U.S. 281/960-7093, www. nicasailandsurf.com, nicasailandsurf@gmail. com, $75 pp) offers a popular afternoon sunset cruise with open bar and snorkeling to Playa Blanca and back on a catamaran. Check their website to join a trip or schedule your own. **Secret Cove Sailing Adventures** (secret-covesailingadventures.com, $50 pp), run by the inn of the same name, offer afternoon trips to the calm, remote Playa Blanca, which include lunch and snacks. You'll get back in time to watch the sun sink over the horizon from aboard the boat. You can also charter the *Pelican Eyes* yacht (tel. 505/2563-7000, $80 pp, $60 pp half-day) for an all-day jaunt, including lunch on a deserted beach and an open bar.

Canopy Tour

Da Flyin Frog (tel. 505/8611-6214, www. daflyingfrog.com, daflyingfrog@yahoo.com, Mon.-Sat. 8am-4pm, $30 pp) is a 17-platform, two-kilometer canopy tour through the trees with great views of the ocean. It's located just outside town on the Chocolata road; arrange free transportation directly from the company. The **Parque de Aventura Las Nubes** (tel. 505/5816-7205 or 505/5816-7297, Tues.-Sun. 8:30am-5:30pm), just three minutes from town, offers canopy tours, walking trails, rappelling, an iguanariam, and a playground for kids. You'll find some of the best views in the region of Ometepe Island and the coastal beaches, and may even see some monkeys. They'll shuttle you there from town for free.

Hiking

The statue of **Jesús de la Misericordia** (referred to locally as "el Cristo"), a 15-meter fiberglass thank-you note for the restored health of the gentleman who built Pacific Marlin (a neighborhood on the northern side of the city), is easily reached via the gated driveway past the Pacific Marlin neighborhood or the ladder that winds its way from about 500 meters around the rocks on the northern point of the bay. The steep walk takes about 30 minutes each way and leads to one of the best overlooks of the bay. You can walk 90 percent of the way for free; pay $1 to access the summit. For a panorama from the **antennas** that overlook the city, take a bus toward Rivas and ask the driver to let you off at Bocas de las Montañas. From there, head for an hour through the trees and pastures to the breezy and beautiful *mirador* (lookout).

Some 1,700-year-old **petroglyphs** are accessible via a 90-minute round-trip countryside walk beginning east of the Uno station. Consider asking for a local guide. Take a left (north), pass the school, and walk through a gate after about 500 meters; find the farmhouse and ask permission to cut through. Follow the water pipes and the river until you find the stone with the carvings. Continue upstream to the (rainy season only) waterfall.

Horseback Riding

Rancho Chilmate (tel. 505/8849-3470 or 505/8755-6475, www.ranchochilamate. com, $69 pp, $79 pp at sunset) offers popular outings on happy, healthy horses. Cowboy threads are available for all the photo ops you'll have during your trail ride through the forest and along the beach. Stay the night and enjoy a refreshing dip in the pool after your ride. Travelers rave about this place. You can also sign up for horseback riding along Playa Maderas and Playa Majagual at **Casa el Oro** (tel. 505/2568-2415, casaeloro.com, $30 pp). **Da Flyin' Frog Adventures** (tel. 505/8611-6214, www.daflyingfrog.com, daflyingfrog@ yahoo.com, $15 pp) offers horseback tours.

Skateboarding

Rancho Surf (tel. 505/8816-8748 or 505/8959-3820, www.surfranchnicaragua.com, free entrance, board rental $2/hour) has one of the only skate parks in the region, complete with flat bars, manual boxes, quarter pipes, and handrails, and with areas for all levels of experience. There's a skateboard shop on-site. Chill out in the pool with a beer when you're done. It's not in town, but you can catch a free shuttle here outside of Barrio Café five times daily 9:15am-9:15pm. Return shuttles make dropoffs five times daily 9am-9pm.

Spas and Yoga

There are free water aerobics (Tues. and Fri. 10am) at **Pelican Eyes** (on the hill above town, tel. 505/2563-7000, www.pelicaneye-sresort.com). (It's worth going for the view alone.) **Zen Yoga** (southwest of the central park, tel. 2568-2008, www.zenyoganicaragua. com, $8 drop-in, packages start at $35 for 5 classes) offers daily classes in various styles including vinyasa and Yin yoga. They'll provide you with a mat for free. They also offer massages. **Nica Yoga** (just outside of town, tel. 505/8517-7573 or U.S. 805/426-5296, www.nicayoga.com, stay@nicayoga.com) offers daily yoga classes, individual guest accommodations, all-inclusive yoga retreats, and custom packages that include yoga and surfing and more. Packages include fine food, San Juan's largest outdoor wooden yoga floor, and a saline lap pool open to guests.

Find shiatsu massage ($30/hr) or chiropractic work at **Elixir** (next to the Casa de Cultura, tel. 505/8971-9393, closed Sun.). **Gaby's Spa** (75 meters east of the market, tel. 505/2568-2654, massage $35/hour) offers shiatsu, Swedish, and deep tissue massages and reflexology in addition to standard manicures, pedicures, and facials. Both places are popular among locals.

The **Tranquila Spa** (at Pelican Eyes, tel. 505/2563-7000 x310, spa@pelicaneyes-resort.com, massage $50/hour) offers massages, professional skin care, nail care, and salon services.

ACCOMMODATIONS

San Juan's lodging runs the gamut from grungy to luxe. The cheapest *hospedajes* are near the market, Nicaraguan owned, and usually extensions of someone's home. You may not encounter much of a "scene" at these places and a knock on the front door may be necessary if you return late at night. It is safe to assume that nicer hotels have backup generators and water tanks, but you should still ask unless you don't mind the occasional candlelit bucket bath. Note: prices listed here are high season prices (Christmas, New Year's, and Easter). During low season, you have more room to negotiate.

Under $25

There are still a few places around town where you can get a bed for under $10, but they are quickly disappearing. Surfers like to stay at centrally located **Hostel Beach Fun** (50 meters south of Barrio Café, tel. 505/2568-2441, $10 pp shared bath, $37 d with TV and fan, $10 more with a/c). The 16 rooms are small, but the owners are nice. You can rent an ATV (don't even think of driving it on the beach) or motorcycle for $20-30 per hour.

★ **Hospedaje Don Wilfredo's** (25 meters east of El Timón, tel. 505/2568-2128, www.hospedajedonwilfredo.com, $10 with

The Foreigner Effect

From about 2003-2008, San Juan del Sur saw an explosion in foreign investment, property development, and tourism expansion that had no precedent. Old properties were scooped up, hotels and vacation homes constructed, and restaurants opened. Throughout the southwest corner of the country, scrublands were turned into investment properties and gated retirement communities under the mantra of "Nicaragua is the next Costa Rica!"

Then it ended with a whimper. In 2009, amid a global recession and increasing uncertainty about Nicaragua's direction, the mood was sour and the verdict still out as to whether it was all worth it. The wave of investment was followed by foreclosures, half-built properties, and bitterness on both sides: Nicaraguans and foreigners.

On the Nicaraguan side are *campesinos* (country folk) who hastily sold their undeveloped land at rock bottom prices, then watched as their homesteads were turned into multimillion-dollar investment properties. Some Nicas now work as guards and maids at the new places. Others, though not all of them, have taken advantage of the short construction boom. Meanwhile, to encourage tourism, the mayor's office criminalized the raising of livestock and chickens within city limits, which hit a lot of San Juan del Sur's poor right in the belly.

On the North American side are the people who bought land during the frenzy but whose developments have not turned out as planned. In some cases, developers never connected water or power, nor built the roads they'd promised. Others blame the Nicaraguan government for suddenly enforcing forgotten taxes and the coastal law that prevents construction within 50 meters of the high-tide mark. Still others fell victim to contractors who ran off with prepayments and others whose workmanship was circumspect. Many investors have found that, far from being the next Costa Rica, Nicaragua was just too difficult to do business in, and they picked up and left.

The tension has boiled over in proxy battles, one of which was the case of Eric Volz, an American expat who was accused of killing his Nicaraguan ex-girlfriend, Doris Jimenez, in 2006. Evidence placing Volz in Managua at the time of the crime was rejected by the Sandinista judge in what observers called a "kangaroo court," while FSLN-organized mobs surrounded the courthouse bellowing for justice. Volz, who originally came to Nicaragua to edit a magazine called "El Puente" (as in "bridge" between Nica and gringo cultures) was declared guilty and sentenced to 30 years—the maximum—in prison. After 11 months in the horrific Tipitapa prison, he was released and fled the country (Eric Volz tells his story in *Gringo Nightmare,* St. Martin's Press, 2010).

For the moment, it seems both Nicaraguans and foreigners live in an uneasy detente, as some foreigners decide to pursue other interests and some have redoubled their efforts to be part of the local community. To the casual traveler, most of this will go unnoticed. But under the surface, the forces of globalization ensure that the battle between the haves and the have-nots will continue to be important.

Jean Walsh contributed to this story.

fan and private bath, $37 with a/c) is a terrific value. The hostel is centrally located just steps from the beach and has Wi-Fi and an open kitchen. The best way to make reservations is through their Facebook page. Ask for a room upstairs for good natural light and airflow.

On the other side of town, the relaxed Hostel Esperanza (half a block south of BDF Bank, tel. 505/8754-6816 or 505/8471-9568, www.hostelesperanza.com, hostelesperanzasjs@gmail.com, $10 dorm, $25 private

with shared bath, $30 private) includes breakfast, coffee, and oceanfront views. Casa Oro (tel. 505/2568-2415, www.casaeloro.com, $11 dorm, $32 private) is a popular dorm-style youth hostel just west of the central park. They run three convenient beach shuttles daily, undercutting the competition Wal-Mart-style, to the chagrin of the smaller tour operators and taxi drivers. Guests love the daily surf report and travel info, lockers, TV lounge, and free make-your-own pancakes on the weekends.

★ Hostel Pachamama (2 blocks north of El Gato Negro, tel. 505/2568-2043, www.hostelpachamama.com, dorm $10, private room $25-35) is a laidback spot with two locations half a block apart. The larger location has a popular bar and is generally rowdier; both have small pools and similar accommodations. Most nights they have activities including beer pong and themed parties with contests (winners receive free passes to Sunday Funday).

At the entrance to town, Hostel Casa Amarilla (25 meters west of the gas station, tel. 505/8568-9174 or 505/8882-7174, info@bonvoyagenicaragua.com, $10 dorm, $25 private) has complimentary coffee and free bicycle use for guests. They'll let you hang your hammock for $5. If you don't need sleep, Naked Tiger (Km 138 on the highway outside of town, tel. 505/8621-4738, www.thenakedtigerhostel.com, $12) has the party scene for you. They have a beautiful infinity pool with some of the best sunset views in the area. They're a bit outside of town, but they offer free shuttle service from Barrio Café every two hours 8:10am-2am.

Casa Romano (half a block east of the BDF bank, tel. 505/2568-2200 or 505/8788-5920, $20 d) is a pleasant family-run spot with great natural light and airflow. It's in the quieter south end of town.

Find a warm welcome, kitchen, and parking at Rebecca's Inn (25 meters west of the park, tel. 505/8675-1048, martha_urcuyo@yahoo.es, $16-20, all with private bath), run by Martha, who grew up in this house and can tell you about the local lore in English. Posada Puesta del Sol (across the street from Rebecca's Inn, tel. 505/2568-2532, lalacard98@yahoo.com, $10 shared bathroom, $15-20 d) has five simple rooms and gives deals to students studying Spanish in town.

$25-50

★ Maracuyá (from El Gato Negro, 1 block north, 1 block east, on the hill, tel. 505/2568-2002, www.maracuyahotels.com, $11 dorm, $35 d, $60 studio) has the best view in this price range from the highest point in the middle of town. The dorm price is quite a steal for the quality and location. Price includes a pancake and fruit breakfast on a breezy rooftop terrace. They also offer yoga classes ($10).

A few doors down, Secret Cove Inn (tel. 505/8672-3013, www.secretcoveinn.com, rjesq@aol.com, $28 d, $33 with a/c) is a little U.S.-owned bed-and-breakfast with Wi-Fi, free calls to the U.S., and bicycles; they also

the smaller of Hostel Pachamama's two locations

Cruise Ships: *Los Cruceros* Cometh

In 1998, the Holland America Line added San Juan del Sur as a port of call on several of their cruises. The announcement sparked hope in the people of San Juan del Sur, who began preparing their sleepy town to receive the thousands of cruise ship passengers scheduled to disembark.

After years of regular biweekly stops, whether or not *los cruceros* have benefited San Juan del Sur depends entirely on whom you ask. The Careli Tours company, which enjoys a monopoly on the buses and guides who whisk passengers straight from the dock in San Juan to day trips in Granada or Masaya, isn't complaining. These passengers never set foot in San Juan proper, and the few hundred who decide to remain in town do not spend much money in restaurants or hotels. A few bars have made a good business catering to thirsty crewmembers, but passengers themselves don't do much onshore imbibing or eating. The *ciclo* taxis and their drivers that cart passengers to and from the dock are imported from Rivas and few of the crafts vendors that display along the tree-lined beachfront strip are Nicaraguan. In fact, the majority of San Juaneños have not gained a dime from the arrival of the cruise ships and would only notice their absence by the lack of tinted-window bus convoys rumbling past their doors every two weeks.

A new $2.5 million tourism project (underway at the time of research) will allow large ships to more easily dock in the bay, and hopefully will help to convince cruise ship companies of San Juan del Sur's appeal. Concerned cruise passengers should attempt to leave some dollars behind for someone other than their ship-sponsored tour operators, whether in San Juan del Sur or in other Nicaraguan cities they visit. And if you like what you see, come back and spend a night or two.

offer sailboat tours and weekly rates. Barrio Café Hotel (1 block west of the market, tel. 505/2568-2294, barriocafesanjuan.com, $39-59), located above the café of the same name, has eight pretty and clean rooms. The second floor rooms have the better view. First floor rooms are separated from the café only by shrubbery.

$50-100

★ Hotel Villa Isabella (across from the northeast corner of the cathedral, tel. 505/2568-2568, villaisabellasjds.com, $85 d) has rooms with private bath, air-conditioning, TV, heated pool, and family-friendly condos ($175, 6 people). This pristine, 13-room bed-and-breakfast is two minutes from the beach and offers business services, full wheelchair accessibility, and free calls to the United States and Europe. Their breakfast is no meager continental affair: homemade waffles, cinnamon rolls, banana pancakes, breakfast burritos, fresh fruit, and great coffee.

Royal Chateau Hotel (1 block east of the market, tel. 505/2568-2551, www.hotelroyalchateau.com, $50-98) is Nica-owned, and their friendliness, the security of the compound, private parking, a big wooden porch with traditional adobe-tiled roof, and a filling breakfast make the Royal Chateau an easy pick. Hotel Colonial (half a block from the park, tel. 505/2568-2539, www.hotel-nicaragua.com, $48 s, $54 d, includes breakfast) has 12 rooms and decent parking. The lush interior garden is a lovely place to relax.

★ La Posada Azul (half a block east of BDF bank, tel. 505/2568-2524, www.laposadaazul.com, $46-64 d) has lovely rooms and a small pool. Tasteful decor, lazily spinning wicker ceiling fans, and classy wood-grained ambience echo the remodeled building's 100-year history. La Dolce Vita (1 block west of Uno, tel. 505/2568-2649, ladoclevita.sjs@gmail.com, $45-100, includes breakfast) is located near the entrance to town and has private rooms with air-conditioning and TV set around a pleasant open-air patio. Ask about free movie nights on the rooftop terrace.

Over $100

Pelican Eyes Hotel and Resort (on the hill

above town, tel. 505/2563-7000, www.pelican-eyesresort.com, $130-500) was one the first high-end resorts of its kind in Nicaragua, offering fully equipped homes with kitchenettes and outdoor decks. Despite ongoing property disputes and management changes, the place trucks on. There are two bars, a world-class restaurant, and three infinity pools overlooking the ocean. Their **Bistro La Canoa** is one of the best places in town to enjoy a sunset. Go for happy hour, otherwise a margarita can set you back $7. There's also an on-site spa and sailboat to charter.

The oceanfront boutique **Hotel Alcazar** (150 meters north of El Timón, tel. 505/2568-2075, hotelalcazarnicaragua.com, $90-149) is aesthetically pleasing in every sense. Each room has unique decor. Services include in-room spa treatments, tour organization, laundry services, and free coffee and tea. Expect luxurious wooden lounge chairs and a front-row seat to San Juan's stellar sunset.

Built in 1902, the ★ **Hotel Victoriano** (on the waterfront, tel. 505/2568-2005 or 505/2568-2091, www.hotelvictoriano.com.ni, reservaciones@hotelvictoriano.com.ni, $105-194) has retained the classic feel of that time. It has 21 rooms, giant four-poster beds, and all the amenities: little shampoo bottles, bathrobes, beautiful lobby, pool, air-conditioning, TV, hot water, private parking, and Wi-Fi. The hotel is located at the quieter south end of town.

Long-Term Accommodations

Weekly or monthly rentals are easy to arrange, both in San Juan proper and in the hills surrounding the city. Most Spanish schools in town have packages combining lessons and a homestay, which can be arranged (whether or not you are attending class) for around $100-250 per week including three meals a day. Most places will cut you a deal if you stay more than a few nights. **Secret Cove Inn** ($200/month) rents a small room with private bath. **Hospedaje Don Wilfredo's** (25 meters east of El Timón, $350/month) rents rooms with private bath

the pool at oceanfront boutique Hotel Alcazar

and air-conditioning. They're always full, so reserve in advance.

For something fancier, see **Vacation Rentals Nicaragua** (www.vacationrentalsni-caragua.com), **Vacation Rentals by Owner** (www.vrbo.com), or **Home Away** (www.ho-meaway.com), or stop by **Aurora Beachfront Realty** (tel. 505/2568-2498, U.S. tel. 323/908-6730, www.aurorabeachfront.com). A fully furnished two-bedroom place goes for $950-1,700 per week and a big house is double that. Nearly all homes come with swimming pools and sweeping ocean views.

FOOD

Fear not the municipal market: you can eat three tasty and filling *corriente* (standard) meals a day at one of the four counters inside for under $3. Evenings, try Juanita's *fritanga* (on the street where the buses leave). Nearly every *hospedaje,* hotel, and beach restaurant makes a variety of breakfasts, usually for $2-3. Locally owned *sodas* (cafés) offer Nicaraguan standards for $3-4. Nowadays you can find any kind of food here, from sushi and crepes to Indian food and Mexican tacos.

Cafés

Expat-owned ★ El Gato Negro (50 meters east of the BAC, daily 7am-3pm, $3-8) serves freshly roasted coffee and good breakfasts, including bagels and cream cheese, in a bookstore setting and focuses on environmental and social responsibility. They are emphatically not an Internet café, but they'll let you use their Wi-Fi. Expect to pay an extra dollar for charging your device. Barrio Café (1 block west of the market, daily 6:30am-10pm, $4-10) makes first-rate espresso drinks and serves breakfasts with coffee and mimosas. They have some interesting cocktails, including a chia and flaxseed martini.

A mellow bar with eclectic music, darts, and a great menu, including a monster Philly cheesesteak, Big Wave Dave's (25 meters east of El Timón, $4-7) is open early for breakfast, then serves bar food and drinks all day long. The ample horseshoe bar is a good place to hang out and chat with your compatriots.

★ Buddha's Garden (with Zen Yoga, southwest of the central park, tel. 505/8321-1114, www.buddhasgarden.net, Tues.-Sun. 9am-8pm, $5-8) serves raw vegan "ice cream," smoothies, salads, and creative meals in a mellow ambiance.

Seafood

A row of virtually identical thatched-roof *rancho* restaurants (daily until 10pm, $5-14) runs along the central part of the beach, serving fresh fish and shrimp and lobster dishes. Josseline's (at the southern end) offers delicious fish dishes, a notable vegetarian soup, and a pleasant atmosphere. El Timón is a longtime favorite of Nicaraguans and tourists alike. Some say it has the best service of all the *ranchos*. It's also one of the most expensive.

★ Bambu Beach Club (from the pedestrian bridge, 75 meters south, tel. 505/2568-2101, Wed.-Mon. from 11am, $7-12) is a Mediterranean-influenced restaurant with stylish decor and cool bathrooms. Serving seafood, sandwiches, and entrées, it has a full bar, relaxed beach hangout with a pool, seaside cinema, and acoustic concert space.

Upscale and International

Vintage (in Hotel Victoriano, on the waterfront, tel. 505/2568-2005 or 505/2568-2091, $8-22) is a classy beachfront restaurant popular for its lobster dishes. Menú (20 meters east of the central park, tel. 505/2568-2063, Wed.-Mon. 11:30am-10pm, $5-12) serves big plates of *comida típica* (typical Nica food) on sleek wooden tables. This is the best place in town to try Nicaraguan classics like *indio viejo* (corn-based stew) and beef stew.

Bar y Restaurante La Cascada (in Pelican Eyes, on the hill above town, tel. 505/2563-7000, breakfast and lunch from $7, dinner $11-20) offers tables set above the village with a prime view of the ocean and sunset. The chef is world class, serving delights such as parmesan-crusted baked mahi over herb spaetzle. Sample from the exotic tropical drink menu.

★ Mauricio's Pizzería (just west of the playground at the municipal park, tel. 505/2568-2295 for delivery, daily from 5pm, from $5 pizza pie) is easily one of the most popular restaurants in town, with great pasta and real Italian pizza by the slice. Ask Mauricio for a shot of his homemade *limoncello* after your meal. Arena's Soda Pizzería (tel. 505/8816-3302, Tues.-Sun. noon-10pm, $4-10) is a small locally owned place with a full menu of pizzas and pastas.

Nicaraguan-owned Sushi la Barra (25 meters east of El Gato Negro, $4-7 per roll) is identifiable by its bright red paint and white "sushi" letters on the entrance. Don't be scared of the hole-in-the-wall appearance, the chef has been well trained, and serves up a delicious sushi roll with thoughtful presentation. Taco Spot (across the street from Sushi la Barra, daily 11am-4am, $1-4) is popular among the late-night crowd and those missing spicy food. (*Picante* does not appeal to the Central American palate.) This is the closest

I've gotten to an authentic street taco south of Mexico—beware the red sauce.

INFORMATION AND SERVICES

From home, check out sanjuandelsur.org or www.sanjuansurf.com, where many businesses post their updated rates. INTUR (northwest corner of the park, Mon.-Fri. 8am-5pm) can provide helpful information on local guides and activities, and free maps and flyers—if you can catch them in the office. Pick up a free copy of *Del Sur News,* a weekly bulletin of community news and events in English and Spanish, at many places around town.

Banks

Nearly all of the nicer hotels (and some restaurants) accept major credit cards. The three banks in town all have ATMs. BDF (half a block from the Casa de Cultura), BAC (in front of Alamo), and Bancentro (next to Big Wave Dave's) all offer similar services, but none will cash travelers checks. Banco ProCredit has an ATM 1.5 blocks west of the market.

Emergency Services

For basic medical needs, the Centro de Salud (at town entrance, tel. 505/2568-2320, Mon.-Sat. 8am-7pm, Sun. 8am-noon) provides free consultations. For any serious medical concerns, plan a trip to Rivas, as the Centro is typically understaffed and crowded. The police station (75 meters north of the port, tel. 505/2568-2382) is on the main beach road.

Laundry

Most of the nicer hotels provide laundry service, as will the inexpensive hotels if you strike a deal. If you'd rather go to an independent *lavandería* (laundromat) with modern machines, Gaby's (uphill from the market, tel. 505/8837-7493) charges $5 per load (wash, dry, fold). There are plenty of other folks with "Laundry" signs posted around town as well.

Spanish Schools

What better place to learn Spanish than at the beach? There are several options in this category. For a full week of one-on-one classes and homestay with meals expect to pay around $250; hourly rates hover around $8. Or, create a custom study plan for yourself that works with your schedule. The Latin American School (north side of the central park, tel. 505/2568-2158, www.nicaspanish.org) is a nonprofit co-op of local teachers who aim to impart social, political, and cultural awareness along with the Spanish language. Veronica's Spanish School (near the Palí, tel. 505/8888-6567, www.sjdsspanish.com) and Spanish Ya (from the UNO station 100 meters north, 505/2568-3010 or 505/8898-5036, www.spanishya.com, info@learnspanishya.com) are both popular options. The Casa de Cultura (tel. 505/8450-8990) offers Spanish classes ($8/hour).

GETTING THERE AND AWAY
To Rivas, Managua, and Granada

The trip from Managua is about 2.5 hours in your own vehicle or express bus but 4 hours in an *ordinario.* From Managua, the absolute fastest option is by express shuttles that leave from the airport. Adelante Express (tel. 505/8850-6070, www.adelanteexpress.com) charges $45-60 one-way, depending on the time of day. Traveling with others will cost you less. For guaranteed service, make your reservation at least 24 hours in advance. Nica Adventures (tel. 505/2552-8461, www.nica-adventures.com, info@nica-adventures.com) also has comfortable shuttles from San Juan to other cities. A private shuttle from Managua through most San Juan del Sur companies or hostels will cost about $80.

Regular express buses make the trip to Rivas (2 hours, $3 pp) leaving from Huembes market about every hour 10am-4pm (the last bus is the best). Slow, crowded *ordinario* service (4 hours, $2.50) is direct to San Juan del Sur from Huembes market. It operates

Volunteering in San Juan del Sur

If you'd like to spend some time working with the community, the environment, or the children of San Juan del Sur, there are a couple of options.

The **San Juan del Sur Biblioteca Móvil** (www.sjdsbiblioteca.com), located across the street from the park, is the first lending library in Nicaragua, a country largely devoid of libraries that loan out books. They serve as the town library and also bring books to 31 outlying communities. Besides helping monetarily, voluntourists can teach English, organize books, read to youngsters, or join staff on a visit to a rural school. A formal volunteer program for librarians, library school students, and others is held twice a year. Book donations are always welcome.

Comunidad Connect (tel. 505/ 2568-2731, www.comunidadconnect.org, info@comunidadconnect.org) is a local nonprofit with a bilingual, multicultural staff, dedicated to supporting sustainable economic and community development. They run the Sports Park by the beach, helped start a municipal recycling program, work with real estate agencies and developers to facilitate private sector donations to community projects, run a small business development initiative, and invite voluntourists like yourself to help with their projects. CC can arrange an all-inclusive homestay with a local family, volunteer projects, Spanish lessons, and excursions to their organic coffee farm.

Nonprofit **Escuela Adelante** (www.escuelaadelantenicaragua.org, escuelaadelante@outlook.com) is a new English school that will prepare school-age kids for bilingual high schools. They'll also provide adult English classes to employees in local businesses. They welcome native English speakers who are willing to help with conversation practice, fundraising, and translating written materials.

10am-4pm. The handlers at the Huembes bus terminal can get aggressive. They will grab your bags out of the taxi, push you onto a slow Rivas bus, claim it's an express, and then demand a tip. Read the windshield of the bus and ask the other passengers to verify.

Once in Rivas, you can take an *ordinario* from the market, a *colectivo* ($2 pp), or taxi from the highway bus stop ($20-25) the rest of the way to San Juan del Sur. After dark, *colectivos* don't run and taxi prices double.

From Granada there are several shuttle services worth taking, all of which cost more than the bus but more than compensate in saved time and frustration.

Express buses leave San Juan del Sur from the corner in front of the market at 5am (this is the nicer *lujo* (luxury) bus), 5:55am, and 7am. Four buses stop in Rivas on their way to Managua, leaving at 5am, 5:40am, 7am, and 3:30pm. *Ordinarios* to Rivas (1 hour) leave every hour 6:30am-5:30pm. You can also catch a *colectivo* taxi to Rivas ($2 pp), which leaves when it's full, 4am to 3pm or 4pm near

the market. Tell the driver you're going to Managua and they'll leave you at the bus stop in front of the gas station, and then catch any northbound bus toward Managua (look for *expreso* on the window for a faster ride). The trip to and from Rivas takes 30 minutes by car and 45-60 minutes by bus.

To Costa Rica

To the border at Peñas Blancas, get a ride to La Vírgen in a bus or taxi, and then catch a lift south; the first Rivas-Peñas Blancas bus passes at 7:30am. Or book a ticket with **Tica Bus** (near the market, tel. 505/2568-2427) or **TransNica** (transnica.com) at their San Juan del Sur offices. Also check with the shuttle services.

From the Costa Rican border at Peñas Blancas, buses for Rivas leave every half hour. Get off at **Empalme la Vírgen** and flag a bus, taxi, or ride going between Rivas and San Juan del Sur. The beach is 18 kilometers due west of La Vírgen; taxis from the border to San Juan charge $25-35.

GETTING AROUND

You won't need a taxi to get around town (you'll only see them trolling for passengers to Rivas and the beaches). From one end of town to the other it's a 15-minute stroll. Elizabeth's Hospedaje (near the bus stop) rents bikes.

To travel up and down the coast, you'll need a sturdy and preferably four-wheel drive car or a decent mountain bike and some stamina. Taxi drivers hang around the main road and can take you up and down the coast, but if you are going surfing for the day, you're better off catching a ride with one of the surf shops, or with the "gringo shuttles" from Casa Oro or other hostels. Water taxis operate from in front of Hotel Estrella.

Alamo (tel. 505/2568-2746, alamonicaragua.com), in front of El Timón, rents cars from their lot, including a selection of 4x4 trucks. Budget (on the waterfront, tel. 505/2568-2005 or 505/2568-2091) has a desk in the Hotel Victoriano. Arrange a car and driver in advance by contacting Ricardo Morales (2.5 blocks south of Hotel Villa Isabella, tel. 505/8882-8368, richardsjds@hotmail.com), a San Juan native with a few four-wheel drive vehicles and a great deal of local contacts and knowledge. He'll pick you up at the airport or in Granada.

BEACHES SOUTH OF SAN JUAN DEL SUR

Between San Juan del Sur and Ostional on the Costa Rican border are a number of excellent beaches. The Ostional bus will take you there, if you can afford to wait; otherwise, do like everyone else and bum a ride with someone with a vehicle, including the several shuttle options leaving from San Juan del Sur's center. You'll first pass through Barrio Las Delicias, which includes San Juan del Sur's stadium and cemetery, followed by a fork in the road known as El Container. Turn right here to get to Playa Remanso, about a kilometer down a path infamous for robberies: Don't go alone. It'll take 25 minutes to get there on rough dirt roads. This slow surf break is great for beginners, so

expect to share it with all the new friends you met over beers last night. There's a shady outdoor bar right on the sand where you can purchase snacks and drinks at inflated prices. At low tide, look for bat caves, tide pools, blowholes, and various wildlife. (Don't hang out too long after dark. It gets dodgy.)

Walking 30 minutes south around the rocks brings you to Playa Tamarindo, followed by Playa Hermosa just under an hour later (it's a 20-minute walk from the bus stop at El Carizal, farther down the road toward Ostional). The $3 fee to access Hermosa helps maintain the beach and the bathroom facilities. Ask in the surf shops in town about safety precautions and public access to these beaches. A night at Playa Hermosa Beach Hotel (tel. 505/8671-3327,

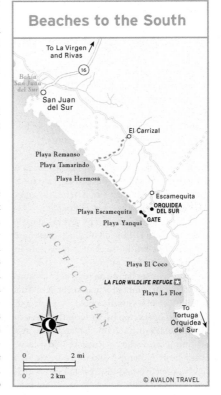

Beaches to the South

To La Virgen and Rivas

16

Bahía San Juan del Sur

San Juan del Sur

El Carizal

Playa Remanso
Playa Tamarindo
Playa Hermosa

Escamequita

ORQUIDEA DEL SUR
Playa Escamequita   GATE
Playa Yanqui

PACIFIC OCEAN

Playa El Coco

LA FLOR WILDLIFE REFUGE
Playa La Flor

To Tortuga Orquidea del Sur

0   2 mi
0   2 km

© AVALON TRAVEL

info@playahermosabeachhotel.com, $18-55) includes free breakfast and Wi-Fi, and they'll shuttle you out for free if you stay more than one night. They offer surf lessons (2 hours, $23) and board rental ($10/day).

A 30-minute drive south of town is Playa Yanqui. This powerful and fast wave that rolls into a giant beach was almost destroyed by one of the new developments when the owner decided to build a "viewpoint" going out into the sea. An effort by local surfers and activists prevented the construction and, for now, this break remains one of the best in the area. Look for a sign at a fork on the main road before you get to the Yankee Beach development; go right and then left at another sign, then over a hill for a photo-worthy view of what awaits. Park ($3) at the small house on a hill at the south end of the beach to prevent theft, or at low tide you can park right on the beach.

Places to stay in this area are limited. Stay in a rustic cabin at Lomas del Bosque (a few kilometers down the road to La Parcela, tel. 505/5840-0022, www.hostellomasdelbosque.com, $3 hammock, $10 pp dorm, $30 d) and wake up to the roosters while assuring your tourist dollars support the local community. Go horseback riding, butterfly watching, and let your host, Don Miguel, point out the various tropical plants and crops.

★ Orquidea del Sur (tel. 505/8984-2150, www.orquideadelsur.com, $175-200 d) is a high-end retreat with a luxurious pool perched atop the hills. Book in advance.

Playa El Coco

Eighteen kilometers south of San Juan, this jewel of a beach is great for swimming, fishing, and access to the turtles at La Flor. This is where you'll find Parque Marítimo El Coco (tel. 505/8999-8069, www.playaelcoco.com.ni, lodging from $185), an extensive compound on a wide beach with a popular restaurant called Puesta del Sol (daily 8am-8pm, from $7). Accommodations range from furnished apartments to fully equipped bungalows and houses. Weekend packages are reasonable for

groups. Houses ($240-280) have air-conditioning, satellite TV, hot water, and kitchen, and sleep up to eight people. Come prepared with supplies. There is an on-site minimarket, plus bike rental, Internet, and a new conference facility. Buses leaving from San Juan del Sur's market for Ostional (7am, 11am, 1pm, and 5pm) will drop you off on the road to El Coco.

★ La Flor Wildlife Refuge

One of the two Pacific turtle nesting beaches in Nicaragua, the park at La Flor (foreigners $8 pp entrance, $18 per tent for camping) is managed by the governmental environment agency MARENA. The park participates in turtle conservation, and will let guests help release baby sea turtles back into the ocean, which is possibly the most adorable thing you'll ever see. Make sure you catch one of the nighttime *arribadas* (mass nesting events) that occur during the crescent moon July-February. For camping here, bring your own gear. Guards offer 1.5-hour hikes ($10 per group) around the reserve, pointing out coastal wildlife and plants. Casa Oro in San Juan del Sur runs shuttles during the season. Public buses to Ostional pass by the reserve entrance.

Ostional

This picturesque bay and community at the extreme southwestern tip of Nicaragua is still more of a fishing town than a tourist destination, but curious visitors can seek out the rural tourism cooperative, COOPETUR (tel. 505/8913-3975 or 505/8498-6650, communitytours@yahoo.es), for tours of the area and nearby bays, snorkeling, horseback riding, hiking, and fishing, along with simple accommodations. All trips are about four hours and have a local guide, whether by boat or horseback. A portion of the profits goes toward 30 university scholarships for promising youths of the community. Buses from Rivas to Ostional pass through the San Juan del Sur market at 7am, 11am 1pm, and 5pm (2 hours to Ostional). They depart from the center of Ostional at 5am, 7:30am, and 4pm,

Turtle-Viewing Etiquette

The Olive Ridley (or Paslama) sea turtle *(Lepidochelys olivacea)* is an endangered species well known for its massive synchronous nesting emergences. These seasonal occurrences, called *arribadas*, take place several times during each lunar cycle in the July-February nesting season and, at their peak (Aug.-Oct.), result in as many as 20,000 females nesting and laying eggs on a single beach.

In Nicaragua, the two beaches that receive the most turtles are Playa Chacocente and Playa La Flor, both on the southwestern Pacific coast. Playa La Flor, located about 15 kilometers north of the Costa Rican border and 18 kilometers southeast of San Juan del Sur, is a 1.6-kilometer-long beach that has been protected as part of a wildlife preserve. Hatchings have been less successful every year. Fly larvae, beetles, coyotes, opossums, raccoons, skunks, coatimundi, feral dogs, pigs, and humans all prey on Olive Ridley sea turtles in one form or another. High tides and beach erosion sweep away other eggs, and once they emerge from their shells, they are pounced on by crabs, frigate birds, caracara, vultures, and coyotes before they can reach the sea. Once in the water, they must still battle a host of predatory fish.

In general, females lay two clutches of eggs per season and remain near shore for approximately one month. The mean clutch size of the females differs from beach to beach but averages 100 eggs; incubation takes 45-55 days, depending on the temperature, humidity, and organic content of the sand.

The *arribadas* and hatching events both occur during the night. Witnessing these phenomena is an unforgettable experience. Tourism can protect the turtles, as it provides an incentive to continue protection efforts, but it can just as easily be disastrous (since the first edition of this book was published, the rangers have been permitting people to "swim with the turtles," an injurious practice). It is too easy to harass, injure, or frighten the turtles if you're not careful. Don't count on park rangers to tell you what's acceptable. Please pay close attention to the following rules during your expedition:

- Always maintain a distance of at least three meters, and never get in front of the turtle. Always watch the turtle from behind. Do not form a circle around the turtle; this can be very stressful for it.

- Do not use your camera's flash when taking pictures of turtles coming out of the sea, digging a nest, or going back to the ocean. The light can scare them back into the ocean without laying their eggs. The only time that you can take a picture of them is when they are laying eggs. The flash will not disturb them as much, as they enter a semi-trance state.

- Keep your flashlight use to a minimum; use a red filter over the lens or color it with a temporary red marker. If the moon is out, use its light instead.

- If camping, place your tents beyond the vegetation line so as not to disturb the nesting turtles.

- Do not dig out any nests that are being laid or are hatching.

- Do not eat sea turtle eggs, whether on the beach or in a restaurant. Despite their undeserved reputation as an aphrodisiac, the raw eggs may carry harmful organisms and their consumption supports a black market that incentivizes poaching.

- Do not touch, attempt to lift, turn, or ride turtles.

- Do not interfere with any research being performed on the beach (i.e., freeing hatchlings from nest boxes).

- Do not throw garbage on the beach.

Shaya Honarvar, PhD, Department of Bioscience & Biotechnology, Drexel University, contributed to this piece.

but confirm with the driver and anyone else you can find waiting around.

BEACHES NORTH OF SAN JUAN DEL SUR

To get to Maderas or Marsella, stop by any of the surf shops in San Juan. Rides cost $10 round-trip. If you're driving, access these beaches via the road to Chocolata, just east of the Uno station. Much of this road served as the old railroad grade for a railroad never built. After seven kilometers, turn left at Chocolata to a fork in the road: left goes to Marsella and Maderas, right to Majagual. The drive out, on a newly paved road through the ex-mayor's cattle ranch, is simply beautiful. It takes about 20 minutes to reach either beach.

Playa Nacascolo

This small cove just north of San Juan del Sur is an hour's walk from town. (A taxi will charge about $10 each way.) There are some beautiful vacation home rentals in this bay. In the hills above the beach is El Jardín (tel. 505/8659-1795 or 505/8880-2604, www.eljardinhotel.com, info@eljardinhotel.com, $65-120 d), a beautiful boutique-style hotel with impressive views of the area. Its isolated location makes it a great place to unwind (and to enjoy French cuisine from the terrace). To get your money's worth, ask for a room with a view.

★ Playa Marsella

This pleasant, breezy beach is one of the closest to San Juan del Sur. You can drive right up to the sand, making it a popular day trip for Frisbee throwers and sunset watchers. On the weekends, a small restaurant on the beach serves ceviche, fried fish, and cold beer. Just can't tear yourself away? Stay five minutes away at ★ Empalme a las Playas (located at the fork in the road between Maderas and Marsella, tel. 505/8803-7280, www.empalmealasplayas.com, $50-85 with breakfast), a small private resort. Monkeys lull you to sleep and birdcalls are your morning

Beaches to the North

© AVALON TRAVEL

alarm in these four bamboo cabins surrounded by trees.

Marsella BeachFront Hotel's (tel. 505/8194-4666, marsellabeachfronthotel.online.com.ni, $49-250) rooms are farther removed from the restaurant and pool areas and enjoy an excellent sunset view, but you can see just as well from the infinity pool. Bed-and-breakfast Casa Pelón (tel. 505/8387-1241, www.casapelon.com, $25 shared bath, $35 private) offers stand-up paddleboarding lessons, surf lessons and rentals, kayaking, yoga classes, horseback riding, sport fishing, and participates in local turtle conservation efforts. To get here, follow the road to Marsella straight to the beach. Casa Pelón's entrance is the last driveway on the right before Concha's Restaurant. Look for the sign. Next door, the Lil' Aussie Hut (tel. 505/8385-6644, www.aussiehut.com, aussiehut@gmail.com, $6 day pass, $10 camping with your own tent, $40 d) is an open-air thatch roof structure with king-size beds that attracts more of a party crowd.

To get here from San Juan Del Sur take Chocolata Road (near the Palí) headed north. After four or five kilometers you'll see the turn off to Playa Marsella and Playa Maderas on your left. Keep left at the first fork in the road. You will come to a second fork, where you'll see signs for the beach. To get here by bus, take the "Chocolata Bus" ($0.76) which leaves opposite the Irish House in San Juan del Sur at 10am and 12:30pm daily. The bus travels along Chocolata Road, and will drop you at the intersection of Playa Majagual, Maderas and Playa Marsella. Then it's about a 2-kilometer walk to the beach.

Playa Maderas

One of the most consistent, easy-to-access surf breaks from San Juan, Maderas is enjoyed for its medium-speed hollow wave that breaks both right and left, best on incoming tides. There's parking right on the beach, and the place turns into a popular hangout around sunset. Surf shops bring groups here several times a day, so you won't be surfing solo. If you're staying the night here, it's a good idea to bring some supplies with you, as there's no store nearby. There's no public transport, but you can catch a ride from Casa de Oro or one of the surf shops in town.

Hostal los Tres Hermanos (tel. 505/8460-7464, manuelantoniocascante@hotmail.com, $10 pp dorm, $20 s, $30 d), a simple wooden bunkhouse with a kitchen, offers lodging right on the beach, cheap meals ($2 breakfast, $5 lunch), and rents boards by the hour.

Matilda's (a short walk north along the beach, tel. 505/2456-3461 or 505/8818-3374, $4 camping, $8 pp dorm, $5 casita, $25 private) has tiny private casitas for sleeping that look like oversize doghouses. The location is perfect for swimming and you're welcome to use the communal kitchen. Buena Vista Surf Club (tel. 505/8863-4180 or 505/8863-3312, www.buenavistasurfclub.com, info@buenavistasurfclub.com, $130 d, includes breakfast and dinner, minimum stay 2 nights) leans towards luxury and is located in the hills above Maderas, from where you can watch the waves while doing yoga on an incredible wooden deck. Mango Rosa (1.5 km from the beach, tel. 505/8403-5326, www.mangorosanicaragua.com, $139 d) has a friendly staff, pool, volleyball court, hammocks, restaurant, and bar under a shady rancho. They've built an environmentally friendly sewer system and are careful about energy use—you'll get a bill separate from your room costs.

Surf instructors Liz and Scott at ★ Rancho Cecilia (tel. 505/8489-9452, www.ranchocecilianicaragua.com, info@ranchocecilianicaragua.com, $65-85 d, minimum stay 2 nights) will make you feel right at home in their jungle paradise. The building has big porches for lounging, and operates on solar energy.

Morgan's Rock Hacienda & Eco Lodge

Playa Ocotál is the home of a much-hyped eco-lodge at the vanguard of Nicaragua's upscale tourism market. ★ Morgan's Rock Hacienda & Eco Lodge (tel. 505/8670-7676, www.morgansrock.com, $268 d cabin) is an exclusive resort surrounded by a 1,000-hectare reforestation project and an 800-hectare private nature reserve. Its 15 elegant, hardwood cabins are built into a bluff above crashing surf on the beach below. As few trees as possible were felled during construction, so you'll have to walk a 110-meter-long suspension bridge through a lush canopy to reach your cabin, which is the most luxurious and beautiful tree house your childhood fantasies ever dreamed up. The structures, as well as the main lodge, which features a gorgeous infinity pool, were designed with all local materials and feature ingenious architecture and attention to detail.

You're on vacation here, so no phones or Internet, but there's plenty to do: sunrise kayak tours of the estuary, tree-planting excursions, and tours of their shrimp farm and sugar mill, where they brew their own Morgan's Rum. More than 70 workers are employed to grow and produce much of the restaurant's vegetables, dairy products, herbs, and other needs. Cabin rates include three meals (lunch and dinner are both three courses), a couple of beers, all you can drink of local, nonalcoholic beverages, and one tour a day. Prices vary by season, so call or email to reserve your room. The facilities and services are for guests only, so sorry, no day-trippers. The resort can organize ground transportation for you. If you have your own vehicle, make a right just before entering the town of San Juan del Sur, at the sign that says "Morgan's Rock 8km," then follow the signs and rocks with yellow "MR" painted on them for about half an hour.

Tola and Popoyo

Ten kilometers west of Rivas is the agricultural community of Tola, gateway to the steadily improving shore road and a string of lonely, beautiful beaches that make up 30 kilometers of Pacific shoreline. The word is out and land prices are rising, but the beaches west of Tola are still far less developed than San Juan del Sur and retain some of their fishing village character. Tola is famous in Nicaragua as the subject of a common expression: *"Te dejó esperando como la novia de Tola"* ("He left you waiting like the bride of Tola"), which recalls the real-life soap opera of a young woman named Hillary, who, on the day of her wedding, was left at the altar at Belén while the groom, Salvador Cruz, married his former lover, Juanita.

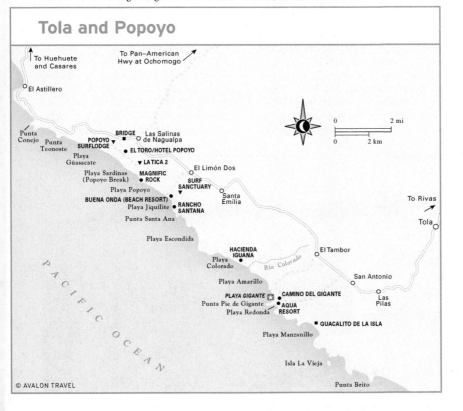

Tola and Popoyo

To Huehuete and Casares

To Pan–American Hwy at Ochomogo

El Astillero

Punta Conejo

Punta Teonoste

BRIDGE

POPOYO SURFLODGE

Playa Güasacate

Las Salinas de Nagualpa

EL TORO/HOTEL POPOYO

LA TICA 2

MAGNIFIC ROCK

El Limón Dos

Playa Sardinas (Popoyo Break)

Playa Popoyo

SURF SANCTUARY

BUENA ONDA (BEACH RESORT)

Playa Jiquilite

RANCHO SANTANA

Santa Emilia

To Rivas

Tola

Punta Santa Ana

Playa Escondida

HACIENDA IGUANA

El Tambor

Playa Colorado

Río Colorado

San Antonio

Playa Amarillo

PLAYA GIGANTE

Punta Pie de Gigante

Playa Redonda

CAMINO DEL GIGANTE

AQUA RESORT

Las Pilas

GUACALITO DE LA ISLA

Playa Manzanillo

Isla La Vieja

PACIFIC OCEAN

Punta Brito

0   2 mi

0   2 km

© AVALON TRAVEL

TOLA

In Tola proper, many travelers have stayed and worked with Doña Loida (an influential Sandinista leader, elected mayor in 2004) of Asociación Esperanza del Futuro (on the road that leads from the park to the baseball field/basketball court, about 100 meters past the baseball field, tel. 505/2563-0482, www.para-nicaragua.de/AEF/INDEX.htm, loidanet@hotmail.com), who can help arrange cheap room and board from a week to six months. Her foundation provides educational workshops to local *campesinos* (country folk) as well as a library, sewing co-op, and gardens; classes in guitar, agriculture, herbal medicine, and computers are offered. There are a few decent eateries in Tola, the most popular of which is Lumby's.

★ PLAYA GIGANTE

North up the coast from San Juan del Sur, and an hour outside Rivas, Gigante is the first beach you come to after Tola and is named after the Punta Pie de Gigante (The Giant's Foot), the rock formation you'll see on the left side of the beach. The community of Gigante consists of a beautiful crescent beach; a few dozen homes occupied by about 800 locals, mostly fishermen and

people working in the nearby resorts; several restaurants and hotels; and a few surf camps. Surfing has had a big impact on the community's economic situation, and it's continuing to grow. Get here before it's so developed that it's unrecognizable.

If you want to spend a week or more learning Spanish on the beach, this is a great place to do it. The beachside Pie de Gigante Spanish School (tel. 505/2560-1450 or 505/8652-7502, www.nicaraguaspanishlessons.com, spanishgigante@gmail.com) provides one-on-one lessons with teachers who have 10+ years of experience. They can organize a homestay immersion with a local family ($100 pp, minimum 1-week stay, includes private room and three meals a day).

Avoid this beach during Semana Santa, when it gets crowded with locals who camp out on the beach, get phenomenally drunk, and run cockfights.

Accommodations

UNDER $50

Right at the beach road entrance, left of where the bus drops off passengers, ★ Cabinas de Gigante (25 meters south of Blue Sol, tel. 505/8667-5498, $10 pp, $40 with a/c) is a great option for budget travelers. This is a

Playa Gigante

quiet, family-run place that offers basic private rooms with comfy double beds and the option for air-conditioning. The family's restaurant is just across the sandy dirt road.

If you're looking for a scene, **Camino del Gigante** (tel. 505/8743-5699, www.gigantebay.com, gigantebay@gmail.com, $5 to camp on the beach, $10 dorm) is the place to be. The dorms sleep dozens of people and are located behind the bar. They also own a cabin, which has private rooms and a smaller dorm, and a B&B with private rooms with air-conditioning. The latter two share a nice pool. To get there, walk down the road towards the left end of the bay and pass the park, then follow the signs. The bar is somewhat pricey, but is a popular hangout spot. They run tours and rent gear as well.

★ **Monkey House** (tel. 505/8255-7547, $10 dorm, $25 d with shared bath) has the best view in town at the top of the rock formation on the right end of the bay. It's the perfect spot to lounge in a hammock and watch the sunset. The accommodations themselves are sparse, but all beds have mosquito nets and all rooms have a fan. The owner rents surfboards and paddleboards and gives lessons ($40 for 2 hours). To get there, follow the uphill road that starts at the right end of the beach, and

take the first left. There's no obvious sign, just walk around the back of the house.

Hotel Brio (tel. 505/8833-3300 or 505/5749-8756, www.hotelbrio.com, $26-65 with fan and private bath) sits atop a hill 300 meters back from the beach, with ocean views and Wi-Fi. They also have two 25-foot *pangas* for surfing and fishing tours. **Dale Dagger's Cool Places to Stay** (daledagger@gmail.com, $18-45) is where you'll find the man himself. Dagger was the first foreign surfer to come to Nicaragua and scout the waves (he shipwrecked here in 1993 and never left), and his knowledge of the coastline is unparalleled. He's got six different lodging options, including a dorm as well as luxury options.

OVER $100

These are resorts on private property farther removed from the community. **Giant's Foot Surf Lodge** (tel. 505/8449-5949, U.S. 562/888-1518, www.giantsfoot.com, from $900/week) rents out two adjacent beachfront lodges with air-conditioning, fan, and private bathroom. Amenities include table tennis, a fire pit, hammocks, DVDs, books, and board games. Weeklong packages include everything except your airfare; discounts are available in the off-season.

Monkey House, Playa Gigante

At **Dale Dagger's Surf Lodge** (www. nicasurf.com, speak@nicasurf.com, $2,095/ week), you get cushy digs, a ride from the airport, all meals, and unlimited trips to some of the best and least-known breaks in Nicaragua, returning to the luxury of air-conditioning, wireless Internet, and running hot water.

★ **Aqua Wellness Resort** (tel., U.S. 917/338-2116, 505/8739-2426, 505/8849/6235, aquanicaragua.com, contact@aquanicaragua. com) is situated in a natural lush tropical forest setting within a private beach cove. This resort, secluded and peaceful, is ideal for a relaxing beach holiday. They also offer holistic yoga, meditation, and spa treatments that nourish the soul.

Food

Some big, airy *ranchos* (thatch-roofed restaurants) sit right on the beach: **Miramar** (next to the Spanish school, $4-7) is one of the better choices. **Buena Vista** (up the road at the top of the hill, daily 8am-10pm, $4-7) has similar fare and is a great lookout point. **La Gaviota** (50 meters from Blue Sol, on the beach, $4-11) is famous for its *plato típico de Gigante* featuring seasonal seafood. **Blue Sol** (at the main entrance to the beach road, daily 8am-10pm, $4-12) is popular for its huge fish tacos.

Buy your own fresh seafood in the mornings from three local *acopios* (storage houses) and buy everything else from **Pulpería Mena** (50 meters south of Blue Sol, daily until 8pm). ★ **Party Wave** (50 meters south of the *pulpería*, Mon.-Fri. 7am-4pm, Sat. 8am-4pm, Sun. 8am-2pm, $3-5) offers delicious sandwiches, smoothies, and even Vietnamese coffee. They also run the only cyber café in town and rent paddleboards ($5/hour) and snorkel equipment ($3/day). Stop by the **farmer's market** (in front of Blue Sol, Sat. 9am-1pm).

Getting There and Away

It's easier than ever to get to this beach town, but it's still a trek. Take the Las Pilas bus from Rivas at 2pm daily (except Sun.). It returns at 7:30am and 3pm. Otherwise, take the Las Salinas bus from Tola or Rivas ($1.50) and

get off at the first entrance to Gigante (30-40 minutes). You'll have to walk a sweaty 40 minutes, or hitch about six kilometers to reach the beach. Taxis on this road are few and far between, but anyone driving a pickup will probably let you hop in back. You could also contract a taxi from Rivas for $25, not bad if you can fill the cab.

PLAYA COLORADO

This beach is widely recognized as having two of the most consistent and best breaks in the area: **Colorado** and **Panga Drops**. The land behind this beach is privately owned, and the best way to get here is to take a shuttle from San Juan del Sur or rent a 4x4. To rent a vacation home from the gated community on this beach, contact Iguana Surf Rentals, who run **Hacienda Iguana** (tel. 505/8736-0656, iguanasurfrentals.com, $375-700). Their fully furnished homes have pools and air-conditioning. They also offer beachfront condo rental ($150-300). You'll have access to the community pool and golf course.

PLAYA SANTANA AND JIQUILITE

Just south of Popoyo, this beach is west of a small community called Limón with just a few places to stay, many of which are closed in October, when the waves just aren't worth it. Take the bus in Rivas that leaves for Las Salinas or El Astillero. Get off in Limón #2. From there it is about a half-hour walk to the beach, or you can hop in a moto-taxi ($4). A taxi from Rivas costs about $25. The 2700-acre resort at **Rancho Santana** (tel. 505/8882-2885 or U.S. 310/929-5221, reservations@ranchosantana.com, $300 d) encompasses five beaches offering surfing, fishing, snorkeling, and horseback riding. Relax by the clubhouse pool, do some yoga, or get a massage. The on-site car rental agency makes it easy to get around.

Villa Jiquilite (north of Playa Santana, tel. 505/8883-8678 or 505/8884-1467, ww.villajiquelite.com, villajiquelite@gmail. com, $15 dorm, $25 d with a/c) has basic clean rooms with shared bath and a small pool shaded by a large almond tree. They serve food from the beachside restaurant.

★ **Buena Onda** (a few minutes walk north of Villa Jiquilite, tel. 505/8809-0794, www.buenaondaresort.com, $15 pp dorm, $35 shared bath, $45-55 private) is just south of Playa Sardinas, where you'll find the Popoyo surf break. The resort is a two-minute walk from the beach, has a beautiful large pool, a mini-halfpipe (boards available), and many other activities like snorkeling and horseback riding. Rates double during the holidays.

The Surf Sanctuary (tel. 505/8894-6260, $60/day house, $1,250/week pp all-inclusive) is a surf camp with restaurant, bar, TV, Internet, movies, and the works. Guests enjoy a private house with four beds, bath, hot water, air-conditioning, private porches, and pool.

LAS SALINAS DE NAGUALAPA

Las Salinas is a humble fishing community. In town, **La Tica** (tel. 505/7855-4030, $10 pp) is a popular restaurant and *hospedaje*. Nearby **hot springs** are worth exploring if you get sick of the beach (ask at La Tica for directions). The springs are also used by local families to wash clothing, so they're not exactly pristine.

Buses to Las Salinas leave from Tola and Rivas throughout the day ($1.50), passing the entrance to Playa Gigante along the way.

GUASACATE AND POPOYO

A few kilometers west of Las Salinas, **Guasacate** is a huge stretch of gorgeous and mostly remote shoreline—beautiful by any standard. The community of **Popoyo** was wiped out by a tsunami decades ago and is technically located south of Playa Sardinas. This whole area is commonly referred to as Popoyo nowadays. Staying at Playa Guasacate puts you near the Popoyo and Outer Reef breaks. The walk from Guasacate to Santana is a good long haul in the hot sun.

Many of the restaurants and hotels in this area are European-owned, unlike mostly gringo San Juan del Sur, and there's a range of accommodations from weekly surf camps to midrange hotels to cheap crashpad *hospedajes*. The entrance to Guasacate is three kilometers down the first left-hand road after crossing a bridge in Las Salinas. The road runs two kilometers more along the ocean until it dead-ends at Playa Guasacate (just 5 minutes from Playa Sardinas and the Popoyo surf break), with a handful of hotels

mini-halfpipe at Buena Onda resort

and restaurants sprinkled along the two-kilometer stretch. If you're here, you're probably here to surf; in case of disaster, take your board to Popoyo Ding Repair/La Tiendita (200 meters before the road dead ends, tel. 505/8464-9563, www.popoyodingrepair.com, board rental $10/day), a small shop that repairs, rents, and sells boards and other handmade surf accessories. Stock up on necessities at La Tica 2 (end of the road across from La Bocana del Surf, tel. 505/8873-0521), a hostel and general store catering to most of the beachfront community.

Accommodations

UNDER $25

★ Hotel La Bocana del Surf (end of the road on the west side, tel. 505/8599-0847 or 505/8391-9118, gerardomena@yahoo.com, $8 pp) is the best value in town. Rooms are dark and lodging is spartan, but the views from the porch are spectacular. They have Wi-Fi and a restaurant on the first floor.

Italian-owned ★ Wild Waves Guesthouse (across from Popoyo Ding Repair, tel. 505/8578-6102, www.wildwavesnicaragua.com, wildwavesnicaragua@gmail.com, $10-14 dorm, $25 s, $30 d, $40 with a/c) has pleasant, well-kept rooms and a roadside

hammock patio. The open kitchen is clean and has complimentary coffee throughout the day.

Popoyo Beach Hostel (tel. 505/8722-2999 or 505/8953-2814, $10 dorm, $20-30, $40 with a/c) has three dorms and a private upstairs room with a balcony. They've got Wi-Fi, an open outdoor patio with a bar, and a kitchen for guest use. They rent boards ($10/day) and offer surf lessons ($30 for 2 hours).

$25-50

El Club del Surf (600 meters from the end of the road, tel. 505/8456-6068, www.clubdelsurf.com, $40 d) has Wi-Fi and six charming doubles with cable TV, air-conditioning, and private bath. Be sure to get a room facing the ocean.

La Vaca Loca B&B (500 meters from the end of the road, tel. 505/8584-9110, www.lavacalocaguasacate.com, lavacalocaguasacate@gmail.com) is a thatch-roof bed-and-breakfast above a coffee shop. Their two rooms have a shared bath and large four-poster beds with private balconies. There's ample lounge space facing the ocean, plus a third-story loft with a lone hammock.

★ Vibra Guesthouse's (next to Wild Waves, across from Popoyo Ding Repair, tel. 505/8322-9065, vibraguesthouse@gmail.com,

Guasacate is a huge stretch of gorgeous and mostly remote shoreline.

Magnific Rock

$30 s, up to 5 people $70) two pretty rooms are simple, but you'll appreciate the attention to detail. Each has a private bath and can house up to five people. Guests are welcome to use the shared kitchen.

$50-100
Hotel Popoyo (left side of the road at the end of a short driveway, behind El Toro, tel. 505/8885-3334, www.hotelpopoyo.com, closed Oct., $50-80 d, includes breakfast, $100 apartment) has a spacious room with a king-size canopy bed, plenty of windows, bamboo roof, air-conditioning, and cable TV. There's a pool out back and a few hammocks slung under the *rancho*.

Magnific Rock (end of Playa Sardinas, tel. 505/8916-6916 or 505/8237-7417, www. magnificrockpopoyo.com, $70-100 d, from $1,295/week all-inclusive) sits high on a rock directly between the Guasacate and Santana beaches, providing a spectacular 280° view. It's popular among local surfers for its parties and live music.

OVER $100
Popoyo Surf Lodge (U.S. tel. 321/735-0322, www.surfnicaragua.com) pioneered the local surf scene in the 1990s. The owner, JJ, is a ripping, born-again surfer who also preaches at the local church. Reservations and packages are available online. Drop-ins (no surf pun intended) are accepted in the off-season.

Food and Nightlife
★ **La Vaca Loca** (500 meters from the end of the road, Wed.-Sun. 8am-1:30pm, $3-7) and **Dutch's Deli** (50 meters from the end of the road, Mon.-Sat. 6am-4pm, $3-7) are the only veritable coffee shops in this area. Their food is all made fresh from scratch. **El Club del Surf** (600 meters from the end of the road, tel. 505/8456-6068, $5-11) features affordable Italian specialties and a variety of fresh salads (tuna, chicken, Caprese) and, of course, wine. For great Italian pizza and calzones, go to **Viento Este** (600 meters from the end of the road, Mon.-Sat. 6pm-10pm, $5-10), which regularly hosts live music and surf movie nights.

The most popular eatery in Guasacate is **El Toro** (behind Hotel Popoyo, east side of the road, tel. 505/8885-3334, $5-10), with an airy dining area and a great selection of meatless treats such as gazpacho, hummus, pasta, and veggie burritos. Rum and cokes are $1 during happy hour (4pm-6pm). **Los Amores del Sol** (next to La Bocana, daily 8am-8pm, $3-12) is a well-liked beachfront restaurant and full bar where you can watch the waves roll in or just enjoy the meticulously landscaped grounds.

Getting There and Away
At least one bus a day leaves Roberto Huembes market in Managua bound for El Astillero via Ochomogo (not Tola) at 2:30pm and arrives at the entrance to Popoyo 6pm ($3). From San Juan del Sur or Costa Rica, you'll drive through Rivas and Tola, following the signs to Rancho Santana, then continue past this development's gates until you reach Las Salinas. Buses depart Rivas about every hour. A taxi to Guasacate from El Astillero costs $7, from Rivas $30. The road to the beach

leads past several austere salt flats, from which the nearby town of Las Salinas gets its name. Ignore the signs pointing to Popoyo, which lead to the former town farther from the break.

EL ASTILLERO AND BEACHES TO THE NORTH

Most of the little deserted beaches in the 10-kilometer strip between Las Salinas and El Astillero don't even have names. El Astillero itself is a fishing village full of small boats and is, in fact, the first safe boat anchorage north of Gigante. North of El Astillero, the road turns inland away from the coast. Accessing the beach anywhere along this area requires a boat and a lot of dedication. Ask around in El Astillero. There are plenty of underemployed sailors and fisherfolk that would be glad to strike a deal with you if you're interested in exploring the coastline. Buses take three hours departing Rivas at 5am or Nandaime's market at 9am and 2pm. They return to Rivas at 7am and 10am and to Nandaime at 6am and 1pm.

Just south of the town of El Astillero, ★ Las Plumerias (tel. 505/8979-7782, or 505/8969-1809, www.lasplumerias.com, $60-75 d) offers comfy bungalows on well-manicured grounds and an infinity pool. Price includes three meals and unlimited soft drinks and beers. French owners Emeline and Etienne are both trained surf instructors and offer surfboard rental, guides, and lessons. Another option is the beachside Hostal Hamacas (50 meters north of the school, tel. 505/8810-4144, www.hostalhamacas.com, $30 d, $45 with a/c). They have a nice pool, but no Wi-Fi.

Beachfront resort lodging can be found just outside of town at Punta Teonoste (www.puntateonoste.com, $164-328 d) in one of 16 freestanding villas. The design strikes a balance between luxury and rustic (guests enjoy the open-air showers). There's also an on-site spa and free horseback riding and surfboards available to guests.

RÍO ESCALANTE-CHACOCENTE WILDLIFE REFUGE

One of the only Nicaraguan Pacific beaches where the Paslama turtle (Lepidochelys oliveacea) lays its eggs, and the Tora Turtle (Dermochelys coriacea), the Torita Turtle (Chelonia mydas), and the Carey Turtle (Eretmochelys imbricata) also lay eggs, is at Refugio de Vida Silvestre Río Escalante-Chacocente (www.chacocentenicaragua.com, $5), a protected wildlife area whose beach provides habitat for numerous other species as well, including white-tailed deer, reptiles, and many interesting types of flora. There's lots to do, including guided wildlife tours to three different lookout points, hot springs and a waterfall, turtle observation ($7.50-10 pp), and visiting local bee keepers ($17.50-20 pp). Organize activities through COSETUCHACO (tel. 505/8603-3742 or 505/8481-1202). Campers can bring their own tent or stay in the research center's wooden bungalows. There's no running water here and solar electricity lasts for about four hours every night. Food from the restaurant should be ordered at least three days in advance. There is also a local group of women who collect plastic bag trash from the beach and weave it into bags that are sold in Managua and online. The project, Tejiendo por la Naturaleza, clears the beach for the turtles and creates income for local women.

Getting to Chacocente isn't easy, which, for the sake of the turtles, is just as well. Take a bus to El Astillero, where you'll find the reserve's tourist center. To get there, the turnoff from the Pan-American Highway is just south of the Río Ochomogo bridge, or take a taxi from Rivas (90 minutes, about $40). Coming from the north, during the dry season you can take the unpaved road from Santa Teresa.

Peñas Blancas and the Costa Rica Border

Peñas Blancas is the official border crossing into Costa Rica. A major effort continues, with financing from the United States, to make this border crossing a bottleneck and entrapment point for drug traffickers headed north. Many of the buildings you see in the compound are inspection points for the hundreds of tractor-trailers that cross the border daily. Needless to say, this is one place you don't want to be caught smuggling furs. Sniffing dogs are common.

Border hassles can last 1-7 hours. The wait is longest a week before and after Christmas, Easter, and during any Nicaraguan election, when the hundreds of thousands of Nicaraguans living across the border are traveling to and from their country. Afternoon is the best time of day to cross. Usually you can squeeze through in an hour.

CROSSING THE BORDER

The border is open Monday-Saturday 6am-10pm and Sunday 6am-8pm. There is a fee for exiting ($2-5) and entering ($10-13) Nicaragua. Inside the customs and immigration building, find a branch of Bancentro, which can help you change money. Its schedule is generally tied to that of the border post itself. If you change with a *coyote,* be sure you know the exchange rate and do your math ahead of time so as not to lose too much money.

A **passport** and some **cash** is all that's required of North American and European travelers, but don't forget to get stamped on both sides of the border to avoid subsequent headaches! To enter Costa Rica, Nicaraguan citizens must have a Costa Rican visa from the consulate in Managua. Upon entering Nicaragua, most North American and European travelers are granted a 90-day visa.

By law, folks entering Costa Rica must have a ticket to leave the country. They usually don't check, as long as you're dressed like you have money. If they do, you lose your place in line and go to the table outside, where Transport Dendu will sell you an open-ended ticket from San José to Managua.

Entering Nicaragua with Your Vehicle

Rental vehicles cannot cross the border. If you are driving your own vehicle, the process to enter Nicaragua from Costa Rica is lengthy but usually not too difficult. You'll present your title *(Título de la Propiedad),* as well as your driver's license and passport. Get proper stamps from Hacienda (Timbres de Hacienda), and a property certificate from Hacienda. Also make sure you have a current tag and *Tico* insurance; all of this can be taken care of in the town of Liberia, just to the south. You will be given a 30-day permit ($10) to drive in Nicaragua. Should you lose the permit, you will be fined $100. Travelers driving their own vehicles north from the border will be forced to pass through a dubious "sterilization process" on the Nica side, in which the exterior of the vehicle is sprayed with a mystery liquid to kill porcine and bovine diseases. This costs $1 and takes five minutes unless the line is long. Roll up the windows and remove exposed food from the car. You can now rent a car with **Budget** (505/8645-4050) at the border. The office is located in the Duty Free Tienda.

CONTINUING INTO COSTA RICA

International bus services like Tica Bus, TransNica, NicaBus, and King Quality are popular ways to get across the border easily and comfortably. In many cases, the bus has a helper who collects your passports and money and waits in line for you. The disadvantage is that the bus won't pull away from the border post until every single traveler has had their papers processed, which can be time-consuming (waits up to 4 hours are not unheard of). More confident travelers like to take a Nicaraguan bus to the border, walk across to Costa Rica, and take a Costa Rican bus to San José, which is often faster. Express buses from Managua to Peñas Blancas depart Mercado Huembes at 5am, 8am, 9:30am, and 3:30pm. Buses and microbuses leave the market in Rivas every 30-45 minutes.

After crossing the border, you've got two choices: Buy a ticket to San José from the TransNica booth across from customs (6-8 hours, $10 pp), with eight departures daily at 5:15am-6pm. Or, get a Liberia-Pulmitan bus to Liberia (2 hours, last bus 5:30pm, $3 pp). From Liberia, 14 daily buses go to San José (3-5 hours); buses leave every 20 minutes to the Nicoya Peninsula and its beaches. You can overnight in Hotel Liberia (tel. 506/2666-0161, www.hotelliberiacr.com, $13 pp dorm, $35-40 d), which is safe, pretty, and clean.

Photo Credits

pg. 2: © Dreamstime.com; pg. 3: © José David Barrera; pg. 4: © 123.RF.com; pg. 5 top: © Daniel M. Hochbaum; pg. 5 bottom: © Cyndi Malasky; pg. 7: © Daniel M. Hochbaum; pg. 9: © Cyndi Malasky; pg. 12: © Daniel M. Hochbaum; pg. 14: © Daniel M. Hochbaum; pg. 21: © Cyndi Malasky; pg. 26: © Cyndi Malasky; pg. 27: © Daniel M. Hochbaum; pg. 28: © Cyndi Malasky; pg. 29: © Cyndi Malasky; pg. 32: © Cyndi Malasky; pg. 33: © Cyndi Malasky; pg. 35: © Cyndi Malasky; pg. 36: © Elizabeth Perkins; pg. 37: © Flor Velásquez; pg. 39: © Daniel M. Hochbaum; pg. 40: © Kate Brinks; pg. 44: © Daniel M. Hochbaum; pg. 45: © Daniel M. Hochbaum; pg. 48: © Elizabeth Perkins; pg. 50 top: © Elizabeth Perkins; pg. 50 bottom: © Dreamstime.com; pg. 51: © Elizabeth Perkins; pg. 56: © Elizabeth Perkins; pg. 57: © Elizabeth Perkins; pg. 60: © Elizabeth Perkins; pg. 63: © Elizabeth Perkins; pg. 64: © Elizabeth Perkins; pg. 65: © Elizabeth Perkins; pg. 66 © José David Barrera; pg. 67: © Elizabeth Perkins; pg. 68: © Elizabeth Perkins; pg. 69: © Elizabeth Perkins; pg. 72: © Daniel M. Hochbaum; pg. 73: © Elizabeth Perkins; pg. 74: © Elizabeth Perkins; pg. 77: © Elizabeth Perkins; pg. 82: © Elizabeth Perkins; pg. 84: © Elizabeth Perkins; pg. 86: © Elizabeth Perkins; pg. 90: © Elizabeth Perkins; pg. 92: © Elizabeth Perkins; pg. 102: © Elizabeth Perkins; pg. 103: © Elizabeth Perkins; pg. 105: © Elizabeth Perkins; pg. 106: © Elizabeth Perkins; pg. 107: © Elizabeth Perkins

MAP SYMBOLS

≡≡≡ Expressway	○ City/Town	✈ Airport	⚷ Golf Course		
─── Primary Road	◉ State Capital	✈ Airfield	🅿 Parking Area		
─── Secondary Road	✸ National Capital	▲ Mountain	≞ Archaeological Site		
─ ─ Unpaved Road	★ Point of Interest	✛ Unique Natural Feature	⛪ Church		
─── Feature Trail	• Accommodation	Waterfall	⛽ Gas Station		
─ ─ ─ Other Trail	▼ Restaurant/Bar	⚑ Park	Glacier		
·········· Ferry	▪ Other Location	🚩 Trailhead	Mangrove		
≡≡≡ Pedestrian Walkway	▲ Campground	🎿 Skiing Area	Reef		
▥▥▥ Stairs			Swamp		

CONVERSION TABLES

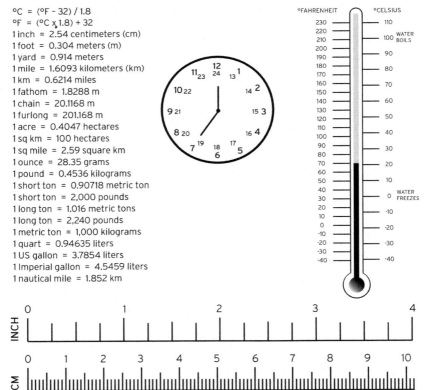

$°C = (°F - 32) / 1.8$
$°F = (°C \times 1.8) + 32$
1 inch = 2.54 centimeters (cm)
1 foot = 0.304 meters (m)
1 yard = 0.914 meters
1 mile = 1.6093 kilometers (km)
1 km = 0.6214 miles
1 fathom = 1.8288 m
1 chain = 20.1168 m
1 furlong = 201.168 m
1 acre = 0.4047 hectares
1 sq km = 100 hectares
1 sq mile = 2.59 square km
1 ounce = 28.35 grams
1 pound = 0.4536 kilograms
1 short ton = 0.90718 metric ton
1 short ton = 2,000 pounds
1 long ton = 1.016 metric tons
1 long ton = 2,240 pounds
1 metric ton = 1,000 kilograms
1 quart = 0.94635 liters
1 US gallon = 3.7854 liters
1 Imperial gallon = 4.5459 liters
1 nautical mile = 1.852 km

MOON SPOTLIGHT GRANADA & SAN
JUAN DEL SUR
Avalon Travel
a member of the Perseus Books Group
1700 Fourth Street
Berkeley, CA 94710, USA
www.moon.com

Editor: Nikki Ioakimedes
Series Manager: Kathryn Ettinger
Copy Editor: Naomi Adler Dancis
Graphics and Production Coordinator:
  Lucie Ericksen
Map Editor: Kat Bennett
Cartographer: Brian Shotwell

ISBN-13: 978-1-63121-225-3

Text © 2015 by Elizabeth Perkins & Avalon Travel.
Maps © 2015 by Avalon Travel.
All rights reserved.

Front cover photo: Cathedral, Granada © Dlrz4114
  | Dreamstime.com
Title page photo: street in Granada © Dreamstime.
  com

Printed in the United States

All recommendations, including those for sights,
activities, hotels, restaurants, and shops, are based
on each author's individual judgment. We do not
accept payment for inclusion in our travel guides,
and our authors don't accept free goods or services
in exchange for positive coverage.

Although every effort was made to ensure that
the information was correct at the time of going
to press, the author and publisher do not assume
and hereby disclaim any liability to any party for any
loss or damage caused by errors, omissions, or any
potential travel disruption due to labor or financial
difficulty, whether such errors or omissions result
from negligence, accident, or any other cause.

About the Author

Elizabeth Perkins

Elizabeth Perkins was born and raised in Louisville, Kentucky. She started traveling in 2008 when she spent a semester studying in the Dominican Republic. Four years later, to the surprise of her loved ones, she packed up and moved to Managua to begin working as a member of the International Team of Witness for Peace (WFP), a grassroots organization committed to developing peace, justice, and sustainable economies in the Americas. As a first-time visitor to Central America, she faced a steep learning curve, but she has since mastered the public bus system and developed a soft spot for Nicaragua's crazy capital city.

During her time with WFP, Elizabeth studied the ways in which U.S. policy impacts Nicaragua and Honduras over time and regularly contributed to the organization's blog and advocacy efforts. Along with the rest of the International Team, she also facilitated delegations from the United States who came to learn about the relationship between the two countries.

When she's not traveling, you can find Elizabeth doing yoga, cooking, teaching her Nicaraguan dog commands in English, or reading a good book in a hammock.

CPSIA information can be obtained
at www.ICGtesting.com
Printed in the USA
LVOW01s1104081115

461224LV00004B/8/P